Experts Recommend Dr. Donald Hall's
Breaking Through Depression

"I am so thrilled that Don Hall has written *Breaking Through Depression*. Dr. Hall has brilliantly and compassionately combined his vast knowledge about depression from his research with his personal experience helping people recover."

—**Paul Meier, MD,** author;
founder of the nationwide Meier Clinics
www.paulmeiermd.com

"Dr. Don Hall hits the nail on the head when he describes depression as a 'complicated problem that calls for a multistep solution.' Don's book *Breaking Through Depression* is a must-read for anyone who has ever experienced the debilitating effects of clinical depression—or who has felt helpless as they've watched a loved one struggle with the symptoms of depression. I thank the Lord that Don has brought his scientific knowledge, theological insight, and years of experience to bear in this important book!"

—**William J. Maier, PsyD**,
Psychologist in Residence, Focus on the Family

"His *chemical cascade* metaphor enlightens the reader on a medical viewpoint of depression. His *SMART model* for recovery communicates an easily understandable pathway to healing. Most important of all, he provides biblical guidance for understanding what is commonly misperceived as a failure of faith…A book full of hope for anyone who suffers from depression!"

—**Archibald Hart, PhD,** author of *Stressed or Depressed?*
Board of Directors, American Association of Christian Counselors,
Dean Emeritus, Fuller Theological Seminary

"Don Hall…weaves lessons from psychiatry and spirituality into a rich texture of insights about the recognition and treatment of emotional suffering. His SMART steps formula is elegantly simple, providing mileposts along the path to recovery."

—**Dan G. Blazer, MD, PhD**, author;
Professor of Psychiatry and Behavioral Sciences,
Duke University Medical Center

"A beautiful book—Dr. Hall has provided the general public with a basic yet profound discussion of the serious illness of depression."

—**David Allen, MD, MPH**,
Author of *Contemplation: Intimacy in a Distant World*
Distinguished Fellow of the American Psychiatric Association

"By combining solid scientific evidence with his practitioner's grasp of human nature, Dr. Hall has provided a clearly marked road map to improved mental health."

—**Ray Linder,** author of *What Will I Do With My Money?: How Personality Affects Your Financial Behavior*

"This resource will be a welcome relief for anyone experiencing depression. The author is knowledgeable, informative, and practical, and he provides solutions and identifies causes that other books tend to neglect."

—**H. Norman Wright**, Christian counselor and author of over 70 books

Breaking *Through* Depression

DONALD P. HALL, MD

HARVEST HOUSE PUBLISHERS

EUGENE, OREGON

Cover by *Koechel Peterson & Associates, Inc., Minneapolis, Minnesota*

Photo credit by *Neil Steinberg*

Clinical depression is a complex medical illness that should be managed in a one-on-one relationship with a personal physician or professional counselor. This book offers suggestions on how to find such a person. This book is not intended to take the place of sound professional medical advice. Neither the author nor the publisher assumes any liability for possible adverse consequences as a result of the information contained herein.

BREAKING THROUGH DEPRESSION
Copyright © 2009 by Donald P. Hall
Published by Harvest House Publishers
Eugene, Oregon 97402
www.harvesthousepublishers.com

Library of Congress Cataloging-in-Publication Data

Hall, Donald P., 1958-
Breaking through depression / Donald P. Hall.
    p. cm.
Includes bibliographical references.
ISBN 978-0-7369-2553-2 (pbk.)
1. Depression, Mental—Religious aspects—Christianity. 2. Depression, Mental. 3. Depressed persons—Religious
life. 4. Spirituality. I. Title.
BV4910.34.H35 2009
248.8'625—dc22

                                                                                2008049427

Printed in the United States of America

10 11 12 13 14 15 16 17 / VP-NI / 10 9 8 7 6 5 4 3 2

To my brother, Keith

Acknowledgments

God provides all we need to live through the next hour of dark mood...or to write a book about depression. I thank Him for providing the healing words and helpful treatments I am privileged to share with you.

I am thankful to my patients, who have opened their hearts and taught me about depression. Doctors learn a lot from their patients. Mine have welcomed me into private moments of suffering and allowed me to share in their days of glorious relief. Although their identities have been disguised, many of my patients' life stories are included in this book. Some may recognize themselves in the pages—other readers, whom I never have met, will feel like the stories describe their own secret challenges and find hope for breakthroughs of their own.

I am grateful to my family. My wife provided comfort and quiet strength through the days of writing and rewriting this book. The delight of my son and daughter refreshed my energy and ambition. My parents, retired schoolteachers, have demonstrated the value of careful study and loving relationships.

Several others assisted with structuring the ideas of this book. Dan Towery's criticism helped to transform clinical topics into heartening discussions. John Peteet and Craig Stockmeier offered helpful challenges to my commitment to scientific integrity. Paul Gossard, Allan Scholes, Ray Linder, David Allen, Pamela DePena, and Amelia Wilson provided editorial advice and support. Finally, of course, I am grateful to my agent, Les Stobbe, and Paul Gossard and Harvest House Publishers for making it possible to put these ideas into print.

Contents

More Helpful Concepts and Tools

Action/Information Charts

A Word from Dr. Paul Meier

Half of all the humans on this planet will probably suffer some degree of depression sometime during their lives. And for many, it becomes debilitating...or even leads to death by suicide or decreased immunity to disease.

It seems that most people think that joy in life is like a light switch that one should be able to turn on or off as desired. But happiness in life is much more complex than that. That is why I am so thrilled that Don Hall has written *Breaking Through Depression*.

Dr. Hall has brilliantly and compassionately combined his vast knowledge about depression from his research and his personal experiences helping people recover. He not only explains the many factors that can rob us of our joy in life, including stressors, genetic factors, and even faulty religious concepts, but he goes on to share with us a series of positive steps we can use to walk out of the darkness of depression into the light of joy, grace, and love. I highly recommend this book.

Paul Meier, MD
Author of over 80 books and
founder of the national chain of
nonprofit Meier Clinics

Hope for a New Vision

D o you wonder if you're suffering from clinical depression? Are you embarrassed over moods you can't control? Are you experiencing normal sad days, or something else? Could it be a physical problem? Wherever the dark moods are coming from, what can you do to make them end?

When I lean back in my office chair and listen, I hear many answers to these questions. A college student remarked, "If depression is a physical problem, then maybe I should exercise." A teacher lamented, "If depression is a problem with the way I think, then I should be able to think my way out of it." The leader of a small group in his church tried praying for several months, then criticized himself for lacking faith and reluctantly asked me, "What do you think?"

I think that normal sad days can wear people down and become a medical problem. I believe depression can start as a problem in the body, mind, or spirit and then develop into an illness of all three. I also know that with good treatment, most people get better. Some need counseling, some need medication, others need a new spiritual perspective.

This book uses models of body, mind, and spirit to describe the problem of depression and what can be done to overcome it. The *brain* models are constructed of cellular structures and chemical networks. The *mind* models are built on a foundation of three basic emotional needs. However, models of the body and mind are not enough for those with spiritual awareness. For them, a holistic model must include the role of the spirit in illness and healing. The *spirit* models in this book are based on problems that can develop in our relationship with God and on steps that may spark revival.

As you read the pages ahead, you will develop a vision of life on the other side of depression, one that affirms your value, makes you a blessing to others, and opens a door to joy in God. You may look back and wonder, as many people do, "Why didn't I see this many years ago?" *You can become better than you ever were.*

PART 1

What Is Depression?

Chapter 1

The Big Picture

*"Come to me, all you who are weary and
burdened, and I will give you rest."*

MATTHEW 11:28

Depression is a deeply personal and complex problem. Sometimes it shows up amid billowing waves of tears, other times in unkindness toward loved ones—but it always brings a lost joy in living.

On the level of the mind, depression is a disabling state of sadness caused by too much worry. On the level of the body, it can be a medical illness caused by injury to brain cells.[1] From a spiritual perspective, depression can present a crisis of faith. For instance, James Dobson talks about the feeling of betrayal that many Christians experience in hard times.[2] This feeling may become oppressive in clinical depression.

Mary Ann, a middle-aged prayer-group leader, came to my office for help with dark moods. She had lost 15 pounds and could not sleep. Her joy in prayer and praise music was gone. She dragged herself to work each morning. Her mind, body, and spirit were aching under the weight of depression.

Her story is not unique. Among women, 20 percent become seriously depressed at some point in their lifetimes (the risk for men is 10 percent).[3] This means that two out of ten women you see at the mall will know what it means to be clinically depressed. Two out of ten women you meet at church will someday be depressed.

This illness affects women and men from all walks of life. With an office located between technology businesses to the east and farmland to the west, I have appointments with both farmers coming in from the field and executives slipping away from the boardroom. It is sadly interesting to see the equalizing effects of depression. Black moods afflict engineers at their desks, the laborers who built their offices, and the farmers who provided their lunches. I meet schoolteachers, international businessmen, and pizza delivery guys who each suffer privately.

Depression is a private illness, a hole in the soul, not often expressed in public. People who appear confident and charming on the outside may, on the inside, believe themselves to be weak and worthless. The sharply dressed stranger on the bus may actually be obsessing over his failures. The woman singing in the choir may actually be thinking about ending her life. Depression is the unspoken illness of the taxicab driver who looks dreadfully sad and the restaurant manager who seems to be doing quite well.

Experiencing Depression

Symptoms of depression are deeply personal and sometimes embarrassing. Some people cry too much. Others pull away from friends and family—preferring to stay alone in their rooms. Food, sex, and hobbies lose their appeal. People stop doing the things they once thought were fun.

For Martin Luther, the great Reformer, depression came with periods of uncontrollable crying. Commenting on Luther's depression, Charles Spurgeon notes,

> His great spirit was often in the seventh heaven of exultation, and as frequently on the borders of despair. His very death bed was not free of tempests, and he sobbed himself into his last sleep like a great wearied child.[4]

For Abraham Lincoln depression came with fatigue and thoughts of suicide. He described his depressive periods as "debilitating episodes of the hypo." In order to protect Lincoln from himself, a friend had to "take away all knives and such dangerous things."[5]

For Bruce, a local pastor, depression appeared in agitated moods. This patient preacher and confident leader became a short-tempered nuisance to his family and friends. With shame in his eyes, he told me about his pessimism and his problem with anger. His black moods were leading to a split in his church.

As I listen to people like Bruce talking about their dark moods, I see depression as a pit.

The pit is deep, and people can't see a way out. They lose hope.

The pit is narrow, and they can't move around. They feel powerless.

The pit is dark and confusing. They don't know which way to turn.

The pit is lonely. People feel like nobody cares where they have gone, and some feel so worthless that they think about ending their lives.

Pulitzer Prize–winning author William Styron explained his experience this way:

> For those who have dwelt in depression's dark wood, and known its inexplicable agony, their return from the abyss is not unlike the ascent of the poet, trudging upward and upward out of hell's black depths and at last emerging into what he saw as the shining world.[6]

After climbing out of the pit Styron told his story in *Darkness Visible: A Memoir of Madness.* Looking back on depression, such a period of time *can* seem like madness. It's hard to conceive. How do well-adjusted people begin thinking and feeling in ways that don't make sense?

Experiencing Recovery

Lincoln and Luther both climbed out of the pit. It probably took them longer than it would today, because without current treatments, depression can last for months or years and recur many times.

Mary Ann, the prayer-group leader, and Pastor Bruce also climbed out of the pit. Within a few weeks, both were enjoying their work and their families again. They thank God for the blessings of counseling and medication. Both continue to do well after several years of recovery.

Mary Ann's contagious joy is back. Her tears have stopped. She no longer obsesses over the safety of her children. When I speak to people who know her, smiles come to their faces. Mary Ann is again leading her prayer group and enjoying travel with friends.

Pastor Bruce is back too, with a positive outlook. His wife and son tell me that the patient father and loving husband has returned. His church is growing. When Bruce returned for his last appointment, he wanted to talk about what had happened—how he had become so depressed and why it had taken him so long to seek help. He expressed some regrets:

"Dismissing the value of professional help really tied my hands in dealing with this stuff," he said. "People are complex, and some spiritually minded people try to make things too simple. They blame their illness on weak faith and think that God only uses 'religious' ways of healing."

Pastor Bruce had been there himself. Initially, he had refused to seek help. He understood that deep sadness can be a spiritual problem and that sometimes God uses suffering to bring us closer to Him. He recognized that God still does miracles.

So he did the right things. He read the Bible. He prayed. He waited patiently for God to answer. He firmly believed that healing would come. He knew that God had a plan.

God did have a plan—but it involved helping professionals. Bruce came to realize that depression can be emotional, medical, or spiritual. Sometimes it's all three at once.

Next Steps

The next chapter begins a discussion of the causes of depression. From the medical perspective, you will see how the *chemical cascade* may hinder the brain from working properly. From the psychological viewpoint, you will see how *unmet core needs* may become roots for depression. Finally, from the spiritual perspective, you will see how six *spiritual flaws* increase the risk for black moods.

Depression isn't simply a problem with the brain—something that, if you take a pill, will disappear. Depression isn't simply a problem of self-esteem. Some people stay in counseling for years without ever talking their way to a cure. And depression isn't simply a spiritual problem. Praying a little harder and believing a little stronger may not be enough to overcome a medical problem. Mind, brain, and spirit may become disabled together. Depression is a complicated problem that calls for a multistep solution.

Moving from depression to spiritual vitality is a bit like taking a cross-country road trip. Before setting out, it's good to know where you are, where you are going, and the route you will take to get there. The next several chapters will help you understand where you are and what you are dealing with in depression. Understanding the problem will help you to develop a personal plan that leads to the best possible outcome.

As you learn about the causes and consequences of depression, it will help you to keep your eyes on recovery. As when taking that road trip, pay attention to what is going on now and, at the same time, keep the road map in mind.

The road map presented in part 3 of this book is what I call the SMART plan for recovery. It can be tailored to fit the unique needs that come with your personal struggle. The milestones along the route are

1. **S**—Stop substance abuse (if present)
2. **M**—Medicate chemical imbalances (if present)
3. **A**—Adjust expectations of yourself
4. **R**—Revise relationships with others
5. **T**—Track with the Holy Spirit

The first step is *stopping substance abuse*. Excessive drinking or other destructive habits can lead to depression. On the other hand, depression can lead to destructive habits. If you continue destructive habits, you may veer off the road of recovery.

The second step is *medicating chemical imbalances.* Not everyone needs medication. Counseling and spiritual commitment often resolve milder forms of depression. However, with longer-term and deeper forms of black mood, do not delay. New research is showing that areas of the brain's cortex may actually shrink in depressive illness. Other new research is showing that medical treatment may stimulate regrowth of brain cells.

The third milestone is *adjusting expectations you have of yourself.* Setting your expectations too high will lead to unhealthy levels of stress. This can lead to hormone damage of brain cells. Recognizing your limits and finding peace within those limits will help to stop the injury and begin regrowth.

A fourth milestone is *revising your relationships with others.* Just as excessive self-imposed demands cause problems, so can unrealistic demands from other people. Learn to say no. Learn to set boundaries. Setting those limits will make room for healthier pursuits, like spirituality.

The fifth step is *tracking with the Holy Spirit.* For the believer, a relationship with God can be a vital part of each earlier step. Spirituality is the emphasis in this final step because full joy rarely returns when brain chemistry and emotions remain unbalanced. When brain cells are rebalanced and self-esteem is restored, people experience a new sense of freedom and excitement that often overflows into their relationships with God and other people. I have seen many believers grow in spiritual vitality as they emerge from the medical and emotional levels of depression.

∞☾☊

As you move through the next chapters, you will most likely identify sources of struggle and conflict in your own life. Recognize these problem areas. They can become parts of your personal recovery plan. By the grace of God, as you examine these problems and follow the map, you too will find renewal of your body, mind, and spirit.

PART 2

Roots of Depression

Chapter 2

The Black-Mood Brain

*"You created my inmost being; you knit me
together in my mother's womb."*

PSALM 139:13

God knit together 100 billion brain cells to form a marvelous fabric of cellular material. This intricate fabric of neurons provides the platform on which to experience the pleasure and sadness of life.

The human brain has the size and consistency of a soft peeled cantaloupe. It weighs about three pounds and is vulnerable to illness, just like any other part of the body. It should come as no surprise that the human brain, which is composed of the same basic flesh and blood as any other body part, might get sick, but it does. Many people have trouble accepting the notion that this wonderfully complex organ does break down in depression.

This skepticism is not hard to understand. Even brain scientists cannot fully explain what goes wrong in the brain of someone with depression. In an effort to understand, scientists have poked, prodded, or electrically stimulated nearly every square inch of the brain. The rest of this chapter is a survey of recent research discoveries and methods. This information will lay a groundwork for understanding how the brain may break down, which can then lead to black moods.

What brain injury can tell us. It sounds odd to say, but strokes can be seen as a natural type of brain experiment. When an area of the brain is damaged by stroke it gives scientists clues about the function of that region. When mood control centers are damaged, depression may follow.

Clinical depression develops in 20 percent of people who suffer from strokes. Strokes in the frontal areas of the brain are more likely to cause depression than those in the rear.[1] (See diagram on page 28.) Strokes in the left frontal part present the greatest risk.

Consider the emotional chaos experienced by one of my patients, an 80-year-old nursing-home resident who had a stroke. Before her stroke, Barbara would talk about her daytime television dramas and tell me stories that showed how proud she was of her children. After her stroke, she shared many of the same stories but would burst into tears in the middle of sentences. Then, with equally surprising abruptness, her mood would brighten, and she would resume her joyful report as if the emotional eruption had never occurred. Her depressed mood appeared and disappeared for no apparent cause. It became clear that an area of her brain responsible for mood had been damaged by the stroke. So I treated her brain with antidepressant medication. After two weeks of treatment, her moods stabilized, her contagious delight in living returned, and her family rejoiced.

Cell loss and regeneration. A shrinking brain is clearly not a good thing. Either through apathy or ignorance, many people reduce the size of their brains through alcohol abuse. This often leads to depression. Stopping the alcohol abuse usually leads to improvement in mood, but it may take a year of abstinence for the brain to recover its normal size. The electrical activity of the brain, as measured by electroencephalography (EEG), can also take a full year to return to normal. A little red wine may aid digestion and lower your cholesterol, but too much alcohol will shrink your brain.

Severe stress, such as the trauma of sexual abuse, may also cause the brain to shrink. One study of women who had been sexually abused as children found that their hippocampus brain region (see page 28 diagram) was 19 percent smaller than in women with no history of abuse.[2] This finding highlights the need to help children suffering abuse at an early age, while the brain is still developing.

While old science taught us that once a brain cell was gone it could not be replaced, new science is showing that brain cells can be regenerated. This ability of the brain to regenerate itself is called *neurogenesis.* Brain cells also have the ability to repair themselves and grow new branches, a process termed *neuroplasticity.* This sprouting of branches and reshaping of brain cells occurs as we learn new facts and develop new habits. Counseling and medication treatments appear to produce their healing effects through this regrowth and reconnection of brain-cell circuits. In the next chapter I will discuss these new discoveries, neurogenesis and neuroplasticity, in regard to recovery from depression, as we examine the effects of stress and medical treatment on the brain.

The cumulative effect of depression. One episode of depression will change the brain a little. Then each subsequent episode damages the brain a little more. Scientists refer to this gradual process of injury and re-injury as a "kindling effect." Just as adding twigs one by one to a small flame eventually kindles a big fire, failing to treat successive small episodes of depression may lead to big changes in the brain, leading to depressive moods that are difficult to control.

Knowledge of the kindling effect originated from the study of epilepsy. People who have seizure disorders experience similar progressive changes. Each epileptic event appears to set up dysfunctional pathways in the brain. It becomes easier for brain cells to misfire and seize. In both depression and epilepsy, early treatment may reduce the number of problem events in the future.

For depressive illness, the risk of having a first episode is 10 to 20 percent for the average person. For people who have already had one bad period of depression, the risk for a second period is 50 percent. Each depressive period in a person's life changes the brain and increases the risk of another event sometime in the future. For people who have had three depressive episodes, the risk of having another period of black moods increases to 80 percent.[3] This progression of injury with recurrent depression should challenge us to treat the problem early and aggressively. Early treatment may lessen long-term injury and reduce the number of episodes in later life.

When clear signs of depression illness are present (like those listed in chapter 11), don't wait. See a counselor or physician for early treatment, and limit the kindling effects of the illness. Even if you've been depressed for years, it's not too late. Treatment of depression appears to help the brain to regrow and rejuvenate lost tissue and abilities.

Understanding the Mood-Control Centers

Mood is like music. Good moods and good music happen when contributing parts are working well together. In a pop-music trio, the vocalist, drummer, and guitar player must each play their part well. If the drummer plays too loudly or the vocalist sings too softly the sound can be disturbing. In mood production, cellular and chemical parts of the brain must also work well together to avoid development of dark moods.

Mood-control parts of the brain are banded together to form the *limbic system,* a long-recognized network of mood-altering structures. Members of the limbic system include the *frontal lobes,* the *amygdala,* the *hippocampus,* and several other regions (see diagram). Like members

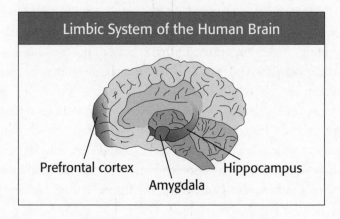

Limbic System of the Human Brain

Prefrontal cortex   Hippocampus

Amygdala

of a band, each brain region must do its part to produce a pleasant group effect.

This is the way of the brain's limbic system. When mood-control regions work in harmony, the limbic music feels good. When parts of the system break down, a person feels sad or angry. Each brain region must be rightly balanced to produce a pleasant mood.

When the limbic system is damaged. The mood-control regions are located primarily in the front middle section of the brain. If you were to cut the brain into four equal slices from front to back, most mood-control regions would be located in the second section from the front. An intricate network connects these parts of the limbic system to other regions of the brain.

Three Areas of Potential Brain Injury		
Area	*Normal Mood Function*	*Change in Chronic Depression*
Prefrontal cortex	Reasoned control of emotion	Underactive and reduced size
Hippocampus	Memory of emotional events	Reduced size
Amygdala	Emotional intensity	Overactive

The first member of the limbic system is the *frontal cortex*, the large bumpy protrusions at the front of your brain. This is the area of executive function. The frontal cortex regulates how much emotion will be experienced at any given moment. It modulates the intensity of fear and sadness. When frontal lobes are damaged, strong emotions may overwhelm executive control of mood.

One small area of the frontal cortex, known as the *dorsolateral prefrontal cortex*, appears to be most important for mood balance. As its name suggests, it's located in the dorsal (top), lateral (side), and prefrontal (near the front) part of the cortex. More simply stated, it's directly above your eyeballs. A great deal of research has focused on this very small mood-regulating center.

A second limbic system member is the *hippocampus,* a long tubular curl that is tucked into the folds of the lower cortex. The hippocampus sorts and files memories of facts and feelings. Damage to this area leads to difficulty making new memories and problems forgetting old ones—common symptoms of depression. Chronic high stress may damage this area of the brain, causing the hippocampus to shrink in people with long-term depression.[4]

The third member of the limbic-system network is the *amygdala.* This area has long been recognized as the seat of anger for the brain. When this small area is stimulated by electrodes in laboratory animals, it sends them into a violent rage. Research in humans suggests that the amygdala may be overactive in depressive states. Anger and irritability are common symptoms of depression, especially among men.

When the brain is working well, intense emotions generated by the amygdala are tempered by reason in the frontal cortex. Emotions from bad events are kept in balance. However, in people with depression the balance is tipped. Emotional responses generated by the amygdala overwhelm thinking processes.[5] Reasoned ways of thinking give way to waves of emotion. Thus, in the person with depression, minor annoyances may trigger excessive responses. When this process continues year after year, the amygdala may "burn out." It may also shrink in chronic depression.[6]

Depression is a biologically complicated illness, affecting multiple areas of the brain. One person's depression may be rooted in the prefrontal cortex. Another person's dark moods originate from other limbic regions. As science moves forward, we'll learn more about limbic-system structures, and a clearer picture of the mood-control network will emerge.

Investigation of the Brain in Depression

Four scanning tools are commonly used today for generating images of the brain:

- *Computed tomography* (CT) and *magnetic-resonance imaging* (MRI) provide snapshot pictures of brain structures, allowing scientists to measure size and shape.
- *Positron-emission tomography* (PET) and *single-photon-emission computed tomography* (SPECT) provide motion-picture displays of brain-cell activities.

MRI scans have repeatedly demonstrated that the prefrontal cortex becomes smaller in people with long-term depression, as highlighted by an article in the *American Journal of Psychiatry:*

> There is emerging evidence that depressed patients have significant cell loss in the prefrontal cortex, a brain area important in...shifting mood from one state to another.[7]

In a three-year study of people with depression, researchers using MRI found that gray-matter density was reduced in the prefrontal cortex, amygdala, and hippocampus.[8]

It's significant that gray-matter reductions were not as noticeable in people who recovered from depression more quickly. Again, we see a potential benefit of treating depression early, before chronic problems set in.

Moving pictures of the limbic system are provided by PET scans. PET scanning identifies problems in function, rather than problems in form. It allows scientists to watch the brain use energy as it thinks and feels. High levels of brain-cell activity are indicated by red regions on PET scans, low levels by blue regions.

In people with depression, PET scans demonstrate low metabolic activity in the prefrontal cortex.[9] The severity of depressive symptoms corresponds to the amount of brain activity that is lost in this frontal lobe area. The bluer a person feels, the lower the metabolism in the prefrontal cortex and the bluer the scan. PET scan studies also offer reason for hope. Research shows that as people get treatment and depression resolves itself, mood-control centers can return to normal function.

A brain test for depression?

It's exciting to see the progress in brain-scanning technology. The hope of scientists in this area is that we will soon have imaging tools to diagnose and guide treatment of mental illnesses from schizophrenia to depression. For example, PET scanning technology has already proven helpful in the diagnosis of Alzheimer's disease.

While brain-scan technology is wonderfully helpful in depression research, these tools aren't yet ready to be used for diagnosing depression. Although not all psychiatrists agree, brain-imaging experts say that there is simply not enough evidence to support using brain scans in this way.[10]

As medical research continues, we will likely have a brain test for depression—hopefully, one that indicates which medication would be most helpful to each patient. For now, counselors and psychiatrists do a very good job of diagnosing depression by talking to patients and their loved ones about symptoms.

Brain Care

Taking care of your brain may reduce your risk of depression. Like other organs, the brain gets sick when overworked or neglected. Make a commitment to improve its fitness by considering some suggestions.

- *Provide your brain cells with a healthy place to work.* By increasing exercise and eating healthier foods, you'll get more oxygen and nutrients to your brain. By eliminating toxic chemicals, you'll spare these tiny cells from injury. Your brain was not created to work in an environment of substance abuse. Limit your drinking and break your addictions.

- *Lowering your level of stress will also be good for your brain.* By adjusting commitments to family, work, and community, you'll create more time for rest. Relaxation lowers the amount of stress hormones reaching your brain.

  Prayer and meditation can reduce stress. Prayer opens your mind to God's way of viewing the world and your challenges. It realigns your spirit with God's Spirit. This peace in your soul can calm your mind and relax your body.

If simple self-help steps are not enough to lift your mood, think about getting professional help. It's not as difficult as you might imagine.

Rehabbing Your Brain

If you break your leg playing soccer, your doctor will realign the bone, place your leg in a cast, and recommend a period of rehabilitation. You won't be able to do the things you did before the injury for a while. Getting back in the game and putting stress on the leg too early will aggravate the injury. If you continue to ignore the problem, long-term damage may prevent you from ever playing soccer again.

Like a broken leg, depression can be a physical problem. If you ignore the injury, a long-term handicap may develop. Therefore, if you have signs of depression, release some responsibilities for a while and get some professional help. This will help you avoid aggravating your injury to the point of disability.

The SMART Steps process I discuss in part 3 suggests ways to rehab your brain and find healing from depression. Some of the steps are specific to those of you with black moods. Others will help those with more common experiences of sadness. Restoring the fitness of your brain will improve the function of your mind and spirit—renewing your abilities to think clearly and appreciate life.

---- **Key Points** ----

- The limbic system of the brain is responsible for mood control. Regions of this network may become dysfunctional or shrink in depressive illness.

- Each episode of depression changes the brain and increases the risk of having another episode.

- Brain scans are helpful in research but aren't yet ready for diagnosing depression.

- Lowering stress, getting good counseling, or taking medication may help repair injured areas of the brain.

Chapter 3
Hormone Havoc

With the flood of time-saving technologies, pressure to increase efficiencies, and diminishing time to relax, stress is taking its toll. Businesses continue to drive productivity in employees by suggesting they "do more with less," leading to increased work hours and less vacation time. Overactive lifestyles put strain on our bodies and spirits. Researchers at the Centers for Disease Control report that up to 90 percent of patient visits to the doctor's office in the United States may be due to stress-related illness.[1] In the book *Blue Genes,* Dr. Paul Meier and his coauthors note,

> Life today is probably more stressful than any other time on earth (except when dinosaurs chased people around). Could this be a major factor in why depression is so prevalent in our generation? Probably so.[2]

The American Psychiatric Association reports that clinical depression affects 10 to 20 percent of men and women in the U.S.[3] The problem of black moods is beginning to affect the lives of children as well. The average age of a first depressive episode has dropped from 29 to 15, leading Drs. Archibald Hart and Catherine Hart Weber to refer to it as an epidemic teenage disorder.[4]

I rarely treat teenagers because I have trouble getting them to open up quickly. But I made an exception when a patient asked me to see her teenage daughter. Tyra was quite open with discussing the things that were hurting her. Friends on her softball team had betrayed her. An ex-boyfriend was stalking her, and she was getting overwhelmed. She collapsed into thoughts of suicide.

Tyra completely recovered with professional care. She no longer thinks about suicide or finds herself overwhelmed by black moods. It's been five years since her bout with depression, and today she is starting a family of her own. Tyra and her mother know firsthand that black moods can happen to anyone when stress is too high for too long.

The Cascade Model

Like water cascading down a series of ledges, the chemical changes that come with stress move to deeper and deeper levels of the brain on the way to depression. What starts as worries related to normal life challenges can lead to unhealthy levels of stress hormones and to brain-cell injury. As large groups of cells become injured, chemical imbalances develop in mood-control regions of the brain. To me, this process is best described as a "chemical cascade."

This chemical-cascade model of depression links several areas of cutting-edge research to show the brain changes that come with depressive illness. A step-by-step diagram is presented on the next page. While this flowchart is a simplified summary of many complex processes,[5] it serves to illustrate how environmental stress and changes in the brain may combine to create black moods.

Where the Cascade Begins

A little bit of stress is a good thing. It pumps up the body and focuses the mind. However, extended periods of high stress can be harmful because chronic high stress leads to physical problems, including heart disease and depression.

Short-term stress responses begin in the amygdala, which senses danger and triggers release of *noradrenalin* (also called *norepinephrine*) throughout the brain. This chemical response leads to improved alertness

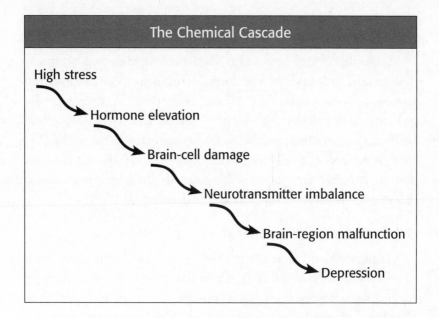

The Chemical Cascade

High stress

Hormone elevation

Brain-cell damage

Neurotransmitter imbalance

Brain-region malfunction

Depression

and ability to process information. Noradrenalin also elevates blood pressure and speeds up the heart, increasing physical abilities—but too much of it causes cardiac problems. Long-term stress leads to unhealthy elevation of cortisol, a hormone that mobilizes stored up energy. While the short-term effects of cortisol empower fighting or fleeing, its long-term effects may very well be damaging to brain cells.

During my service in a U.S. Army Combat Stress Control unit, I was reminded of the distinction between the short-term and long-term effects of stress. I was deployed with paratroopers of the 82nd Airborne Division on a peacekeeping mission to Haiti.

We lived in an abandoned warehouse: 200 soldiers, 200 cots, remnants of cow dung on the floors, no privacy, and plenty of heat. This was living *well*. The medical staff had privileges—a roof over our heads and makeshift latrines. The rest of the troops had to rough it.

During the initial days of the mission, soldiers came to our mental-health unit complaining of sudden onset of anxiety and depression, reflecting the initial noradrenalin response. They were jittery, shaky,

and overaroused, but their depressive moods usually resolved themselves with a few days of rest.[6]

As the deployment continued, this event-based depression nearly
disappeared, but soldiers with longer-term depression continued to
come to our treatment tent. Those with brain-changing depression did
not respond as well to rest and support. Some required antidepressant
medication, and others needed to be air-evacuated home to the U.S.
Within 30 days of deployment, however, hot food and comfortable
cots arrived, and danger nearly disappeared. Stress hormones settled
down, and visits to our psychiatric tent declined.

Chemical Effects

People frequently use the phrase "burned out" to describe their
state of mind before and during a depressive episode. After his recovery
from chronic depression, John, a computer engineer, aptly described
the physical feelings that come with overwhelming stress. Each episode of black mood, he told me, had been preceded by a feeling that
"something chemical was going on...adrenaline or something...it was
out of my control." Either through an awareness of his blood pressure
or changes in his heart rate, or some other physical sensation, John
felt his body crying out.

On reflection, it's quite likely John did feel "something chemical"
going on. As mentioned previously, stress hormones pump up the body
to get ready for a fight, but this physical activation can also interfere
with sleep and create feelings of nervousness. Most depressed patients
do not recall these early sensations, but most pass through periods of
excessive physical arousal on the way to becoming depressed. These
changes mark the first steps along the biochemical pathway to brain-
cell injury and depression.

Damage to Brain Cells Begins

High levels of emotional stress may cause physical injury throughout the body. When people get overwhelmed they may get headaches,
ulcers, or neck pain. As an intern in a hospital ICU, I saw a widow's

tearful outburst cause EKG changes and signs of a heart attack.[7] Without rapid treatment, the emotions could have killed her.

In the brain, stress can cause damage through the action of cortisol. People with depression tend to have high levels of this stress hormone in their bloodstream. Blood levels of cortisol are increased in 30 percent of depressed patients who visit outpatient mental health clinics and in 50 percent of patients hospitalized for depression. During depression, cortisol levels are also increased in the fluid that surrounds the brain.[8]

Excessive exposure to cortisol interferes with the brain's chemical messenger systems, breaking off delicate branches of some brain cells and killing others.[9] Loss of the branching axons and fragile dendrites of brain cells hampers their ability to communicate with each other. This damage may reduce the levels of serotonin, a major mood messenger, thus increasing the risk of depression.

Toxic Effects of Cortisol on Brain Cells

- Snipping off of cell branches
- Impairment of serotonin function
- Blocking of cell growth
- Cell death

Another link between stress hormone and depression comes from the experience of patients taking prednisone, a man-made form of cortisol. Prednisone mimics both the good and bad effects of the hormone. It is frequently used to treat arthritis, allergic reactions, and other conditions requiring strong anti-inflammatory action. In small doses prednisone liberates energy and reduces inflammation, but with extended use it may cause obesity and problems managing emotions.

People can get horribly depressed on prednisone. Within two weeks of starting to take it, one mild-tempered schoolteacher plummeted into a suicidal depression. Because of the severity of her asthma, she needed to continue the medication despite her worsening depression. As her mood and thoughts became more disturbed, she began to fantasize about killing her husband with a kitchen knife. In daylight hours, her moods shifted between depression and rage. At night, nightmares carried her to tormenting visions of hell. When she stopped the medication, her thoughts reorganized themselves and her depression lifted. For her, prednisone was depression in a pill. Sadly, the severity of her asthma made it necessary that she repeat using prednisone many times over the years. Each time, depressive moods came and went as she started and then stopped the man-made cortisol.

Potential Toxic Effects of Cortisol on Mood

- Agitation
- Manic excitement
- Rage
- Depression
- Suicidal thoughts

Recognizing this link between cortisol and depression, some people have suggested using cortisol blood tests to diagnose depression. One of my well-read clients recently asked for one. Unfortunately, such tests offer little real value in diagnosing or treating depression.

Nonetheless, nutrient-supplement companies jumped on this new science and have used the information to sell cortisol-blocking supplements. This is not a good idea. Such supplements have not been proven to help or to be safe for public use. Although pharmaceutical companies are working on cortisol-altering cures, we are years away from hormone-blocking medication that helps with depression.

Brain Growth Factors

Even though high levels of stress hormones may tear down brain cells, helpful natural chemicals are working to build them up. These revitalizing agents are known as *growth factors.* They circulate between brain cells, stimulating the repair of damaged cells and promoting the health of others. In some regions, growth factors even spark neurogenesis, the creation of new brain cells.

One of these growth factors is *BDNF* (brain-derived neurotrophic factor). BDNF is beneficial and nurturing. It comes alongside damaged brain cells to repair the injuries caused by stress and daily activity. However, in someone suffering prolonged distress, stress hormones repress production of this rejuvenating agent. The harsh effects of cortisol on the brain may be due to its interference with BDGF. Too much cortisol gets in the way of the care and feeding of brain cells.

Some scientists have suggested that repressed levels of growth factors combined with brain-cell death may cause depression.[10] Others have found that the more severe the symptoms of depression, the lower a person's levels of these growth factors will be—more evidence that growth-factor impairment is linked to low mood.[11]

Further evidence for a link between growth factors and depression comes from research on antidepressant drugs. Studies show that antidepressant medication may increase the level of growth factor during the course of recovery.[12] In summary, while prolonged exposure to stress hormones appears to trigger depressive illness through repression of growth factor, antidepressants may treat depression by elevating growth factor and promoting the repair of brain tissue. (When I described these fertilizer effects of antidepressants to one of my lighthearted patients, she replied, "Well, I feel like a flower," and laughed.)

Thyroid and Sex-Hormone Effects

A number of biological problems can disturb brain-cell balance and hasten the onset of depression. Illness in other areas of the body and medication side effects can have profound effects on mood. And hormone imbalances in the thyroid and ovaries are two potent triggers for the illness of black moods.

Approximately 5 percent of people diagnosed with depression have abnormally low levels of thyroid hormone.[13] Thyroid-hormone imbalances can lead to low energy, reduced motivation, and sleep disruptions that look like clinical depression. When hormone levels are corrected with thyroid supplements, many people find relief from depression. Others also require antidepressant medication.

Sex-hormone fluctuations can also have a big effect on mood. Postpartum depression is an example. Similar problems may occur with the hormonal shifts that come with premenstrual syndrome and menopause. Birth-control medications, which are man-made combinations of hormones produced by the ovaries, are also potential triggers of depression. The brain cells of some women are exquisitely sensitive to fluctuations in these reproductive hormones.

A choir director I treated for severe depression reported the onset of a ten-year depressive period after a brief use of birth-control medication. Many times, this otherwise spiritually mature woman wished to be dead. Her black moods disappeared when she found the right antidepressant medication.

⁦⁧

In meeting with patients at my office, I haven't yet asked anyone, "How are your brain cells doing today?" I must admit, however, this is often what I'm thinking as we talk about symptoms of depression. In many cases, the person walking through my doorway brings with him or her a brain that has been challenged by years of stressful situations and stress hormones. Between their tearfulness and descriptions of lost joy in living, I consider the possible physical injuries. In caring for those with black moods, I empathize with the soul in anguish—but I begin treatment with attention to those brain cells.

--- **Key Points** ---

- High levels of stress that continue for a long time can damage the delicate branches of brain cells.
- The feeling of burnout may be a sign of an impending depressive episode.
- The brain has a natural ability to heal itself. New research is likely to show that counseling, faith, medication, and the simple passing of time may each play a role in this healing process.
- Stress hormones like cortisol may interfere with natural processes of brain-cell healing.
- The brain's own growth factors, including BDNF, help cells repair their broken parts.
- The brain can actually grow new brain cells, a process called *neurogenesis*.
- Nutrient supplements that are advertised to correct hormone imbalances appear to make sense, but are not proven helpful or safe for treatment of depression.

Chapter 4

Mood-Messenger Misfire

The most powerful way to change a person's mood is through chemical stimulation of brain cells. Drugs that are abused do this in a manner that causes intoxication and dependence. Antidepressant medications do it without the intoxicating effects or risk of addiction. While drugs that are abused produce chemical imbalances and short-term elevations in mood, antidepressants correct chemical imbalances and restore normal moods.

These chemical changes in the brain are best explained by looking at neurotransmitters (NTs), the "messengers of mood." NTs are the chemical messengers of the brain. They allow cells to communicate with each other. For one cell to send a message to its neighboring cell, it must release a neurotransmitter. When this chemical messenger reaches the neighbor, it attaches itself to that cell like a key going into the ignition of an automobile. With this attachment, the NT stimulates the next cell to start performing its functions.

Three NTs are critically important to mood-control functions. These are *serotonin, norepinephrine,* and *dopamine.* The illness of depression can be caused by imbalance in one or all three of these mood messengers. The specific type of depressive symptoms experienced by each person may depend on which NT system is out of balance.

The discovery of this relationship between brain NTs and mood control occurred quite by accident. Doctors who were treating other illnesses found that their medications were causing side effects on mood. One medication that was used to treat high blood pressure (reserpine) caused patients to develop depression so severe that they required psychiatric hospitalization. Reserpine causes this depression by depleting the level of brain NTs. Another medicine (isoniazid), used to treat tuberculosis, had the opposite side effect. Isoniazid helped people recover from tuberculosis but caused mood-elevating side effects by increasing NTs.[1]

The following information on serotonin, norepinephrine, and dopamine point to special functions for each of these NTs. These observations are based on clinical experience with antidepressant medication, not controlled experiments. Even so, these clinical observations help us appreciate the varieties of NT imbalances that may occur in depression and the medical approaches to treatment that are used. While all antidepressants produce mood elevation, those which stimulate one NT more than another may be better suited for specific types of depression.

Serotonin

Serotonin stimulation of brain cells causes a relaxation response. Therefore, antidepressants that enhance serotonin tend to be better for decreasing worry, controlling irritability, and promoting normal sleep. Some scientists have suggested that serotonin neurotransmitters may also play a role in spirituality.[2]

Sally came to my office with complaints of not getting enough sleep. She lay awake for most of the night, obsessively worrying about her grandson. She was becoming impatient with co-workers and friends, and she felt guilty about her emotional outbursts. She felt spiritually cold and separated from God. So we talked about counseling, medication, and spiritual supports and then decided to begin treatment with a serotonergic antidepressant.

Within two weeks, the boost in serotonin neurotransmission began to restore Sally's brain function and her sense of well-being. Yelling at her children and petty arguments with co-workers ended. She was less irritable in the daytime, and when her head hit the pillow at night, she enjoyed eight hours of restorative sleep. Her spiritual vitality returned as she found new meaning in Scripture and spiritual connection in prayer.

Norepinephrine

The second neurotransmitter associated with mood regulation is norepinephrine (also called noradrenalin). While it is delivering messages of good mood to brain cells, this messenger also increases mental energy. When norepinephrine is low, depression may be marked by apathy and lost motivation—an unwillingness to get off the couch and get on with life. Antidepressants that target norepinephrine may be the best for recovering that lost energy.

Nancy was on short-term disability for deep depression and fatigue. She could not keep up with the students in her special-education classroom. When she tried to return to work too early, she paid a great price. She was unable to keep order in the classroom and embarrassed herself in front of her co-workers and students.

Nancy took an antidepressant that increases norepinephrine. It took a few weeks, but she got back in the classroom with new energy and alertness. Rebalance of norepinephrine relieved her low-energy depression. She is now investing this new vigor in psychotherapy, learning about mental and spiritual tools that can be used to keep her brain cells and her life in better balance.

Mood-Messenger Functions (clinical observations)		
Neurotransmitter	*Function*	*Dysfunction*
Serotonin	Sleep Calming	Irritability Worry
Norepinephrine	Energy Alertness	Apathy Dullness
Dopamine	Pleasure Concentration	Addiction Distraction

Dopamine

The third member of the mood-messenger trio is dopamine. Many pleasurable experiences exert their effect on the brain through the dopamine system. When dopamine levels are low, people complain of *anhedonia* (absence of pleasure). They can't find pleasure in hobbies, food, or sex—common complaints of people stuck in depression.

Dopamine also improves mental focus. People with dopamine-deficit depression may have trouble balancing a checkbook or finishing a magazine article. When depression comes with serious concentration problems, I think about a dopamine-enhancing medication because this neurotransmitter both lifts the mood and focuses attention.

The dopamine system also plays a role in addictive behaviors. Addictions to drugs, sex, and cigarettes develop through dopamine stimulation of the *nucleus accumbens* region of the brain. One medication (bupropion) boosts dopamine activity and has been approved by the FDA for treating nicotine dependence. It may also be helpful in managing other addictions.

Dan was a tax accountant, so it was important for him to stay focused on details. When he got depressed, dark moods came with serious problems in concentration. He had trouble organizing his responsibilities at work and keeping focused on the book he was reading in the evening.

Something always seemed distracting—the voices of his co-workers, the ring of a phone, or thoughts about tomorrow's special meeting. He couldn't keep his mind focused on what was in front of him. We talked about the various types of medication for depression with profound concentration deficits.

Dan took a dopamine-stimulating antidepressant. His ability to focus on tasks and manage his schedule improved over the next two weeks. His accounting performance is top-notch again. He can stay focused on the pages of his military-history novels and spending meaningful time with his family. He's happy that the medication has restored his emotional balance and optimized his concentration abilities.

Receptors for Neurotransmitters

If neurotransmitter molecules act like keys in the ignition, then receptors are like keyholes. When an NT is released from one brain cell, it travels across a small gap and attaches to the receptor of a neighboring brain cell, activating chemical and electrical activity within that cell. Most medications work by either blocking the keyhole so NTs can't attach, or by acting like copies of the key, mimicking action of the NT.

Depression in the laboratory

Before medical school I worked with a group of scientists at Georgetown University studying receptors for mood-messenger NTs. We used animals to study the effects of antidepressants on NT receptors.

My job was to treat a group of white rats with reserpine to deplete their mood-control neurotransmitters and create a chemically induced depression. I removed their brains and tested them for NT receptor changes. "Depression" in the rats produced an increased number of serotonin, norepinephrine, and dopamine receptors. Next, I treated the "depressed" rats with antidepressants. Examination then revealed that the number of receptors went back down. Depletion of mood-control NTs made the receptors go up, and antidepressant treatment brought them back to normal again.

Experiments like the one I describe above demonstrate the delicate balance between neurotransmitters and their receptors. When NTs are low, the body makes more receptors. Sometimes this compensation is enough to keep communication going. At other times, the increased number of receptors don't restore sufficient chemical messaging. For times like these, outside chemical help (medication) may be needed to restore function.

Since our days in the animal lab, one scientist from the group has moved to the study of the brains of people who have died with depression. Using autopsy samples, he has found that serotonin receptors are increased in some of these people.[3] He is careful to explain that these receptor changes are only part of the problem. Depression is not a "simple chemical imbalance," he adamantly emphasizes. There are numerous brain changes that are being identified in people who have died in black moods.

The brain was created with a delicate balance of NTs and NT receptors, and these NT-receptor systems are controlled by a host of chemical and cellular processes. The takeaway message, however, is that both NTs and NT receptors are potential sources of brain-cell malfunction in depression.

The good news is that receptor problems can be corrected by antidepressant medication and probably by nonmedical treatments. Antidepressants work by increasing mood NT activity, improving the function of sluggish brain cells, and returning receptor levels to normal.

Spiritual Receptors?

Is there a part of the brain that lets spirituality in? Could it be that specific brain molecules facilitate spiritual experience? Some scientists suggest that the serotonin system is uniquely structured to facilitate spiritual awareness. Research on the subject is very preliminary but quite thought-provoking.

One research study, using PET scans of the brain, found that people who reported more spiritual experiences had more serotonin-receptor binding than people who did not report such experiences.[4] This intriguing finding needs further research because the study didn't distinguish between people with religious spirituality from those with nonreligious experiences; nor did it examine the role of depression. Further research is also needed to show if serotonin receptor activity is more important than other NT receptors in facilitating spiritual awareness.

In my experience, most religious people feel less spiritually aware during periods of clinical depression. Their spiritual vitality usually returns to normal after treatment of depression, whether medical or nonmedical. Renewal of spiritual vitality appears to be a common benefit to all antidepressants, not only the ones which stimulate serotonin receptors. Each type of antidepressant helps to restore enjoyment of life's pleasures, including food, sex, relationships with others, and relationship with God. Mystical-biological connections aside, healthy NT function enables a spiritually aware person to enjoy spirituality in the same way it helps him or her enjoy a relationship with a friend.

Reversing Mood-Messenger Misfire

Movement down the chemical cascade from stress to depression may be sped up or slowed down depending on your responses to life's challenges. Disregarding the signs of stress, misusing alcohol, or isolating yourself from those who can help will speed up the process. Healthier choices, such as finding a less demanding job, getting good counsel, or seeking spiritual growth will reduce stress-hormone levels and help to stabilize your mood.

The SMART Steps model described in part 3 will suggest tools to reverse many of the chemical changes associated with depressive darkness. As I indicated, in moderate depression, counseling and spiritual pursuits may restore the chemical balance of your brain cells. For more serious forms of depression, medication may be needed. Chapter 14 will walk you through a discussion of potential risks and benefits of activating mood-control circuits with medication.

Sometimes God heals through prayers of faith; sometimes through the words of counselors. At other times, He uses physicians and medication to restore healthy brain-cell function and renew our abilities to love and to work. Because He is the God of the cosmos, He is also the God of neurotransmitters and brain-growth factors. He can restore your brain chemistry in whatever way He chooses.

Key Points

- Multiple levels of brain-chemistry function may be altered in depression.
- Depression may be caused by chemical imbalances in

neurotransmitters, in particular serotonin, norepinephrine, and dopamine.

- Neurotransmitters and their receptors work like a key in an automobile ignition, starting up the chemical activity of brain cells.
- Medical research demonstrates that stimulating neurotransmitter receptors with antidepressants rebalances brain chemistry and relieves specific symptoms of depression.
- Further research is likely to show that similar brain-chemistry alterations occur with counseling, spiritual growth, and other measures that improve stress management.

Chapter 5

The Inheritance of Dark Moods

"I praise you because I am fearfully and wonderfully made; your works are wonderful, I know that full well."

PSALM 139:14

The creative power of God is wonderfully displayed in a tapestry of genetic material resting inside each cell of your body. The threads of this tapestry are chromosomes, stringlike collections of genes. Each little gene along the strand is a packet of information that describes how to build everything from toenails to brain cells.

Chromosomes are God's blueprints. When God created man, He included a perfectly crafted set of blueprints inside every cell. With the passage of time and passing of chromosomes down through many generations, errors have developed in copies of the blueprints.

When blueprints for a house are copied incorrectly, problems in construction may result. Consequently, walls may crack under their load. Windows and doors may not open and close correctly. When chromosome blueprints are copied incorrectly, cells may become chemically imbalanced. Thinking gets fuzzy, and emotions become overwhelming. These changes in chromosomes are permanent. The brain-construction errors can be passed on to children, increasing their risk for such illness.

Discovering the Genes of Depression

Scientists are beginning to find clues to the origin of depression in genes. There are at least 30,000 genes to examine, but the gene of greatest interest today is the one that holds directions for constructing a serotonin transport system. The serotonin transport system is important for getting serotonin transmitters back into brain cells after they're used as messengers in brain-cell communication.

Just like a cell phone must be replenished with power after hours of conversation, brain cells must be replenished with serotonin. If the gene that guides construction of the serotonin transporter (replenisher) is defective, the transporter itself will malfunction. It becomes hard to recharge brain cells, and communication along cellular pathways gets weak. This helps to explain the sluggish feelings and muddled thinking that comes with black moods.

The gene for the serotonin transporter is located on chromosome 17 and comes in two forms: a short form and a long form. The shorter version contains blueprint errors for building the transporter system. People who inherit the short form of this gene will have problems transporting serotonin into their brain cells. This construction error makes them more vulnerable to stress and more likely to develop depressive disorders. On the other hand, people who inherit the long form of the gene code will build a healthy transporter and recharge their brain cells more effectively, thus avoiding depression.[1]

As with other illnesses, depression is probably not caused by a single gene problem. More study is likely to find that multiple gene defects plus high levels of stress are necessary to trigger the illness of black moods.

Family Patterns of Inheritance

Further evidence for the genetic basis of depression comes from the study of family inheritance patterns. The average risk for someone in the United States developing clinical depression at some point in his lifetime is 10 percent for men and 20 percent for women. However, the risk of depression doubles if the child's parent has depression, going from 10 percent to 20 percent for male children and from 20 percent up to 40 percent for female children.[2]

The importance of family genetics in determining depression is even more substantial in bipolar depression. While the risk of developing bipolar disorder is about 1 percent in the general community, that risk jumps to 10 percent (a tenfold increase) if one of your parents has the illness. This figure of 10 percent is disheartening, but it is also reassuring to note that 90 percent of children with one parent with bipolar disorder will *not* develop the illness.

Inheritance Patterns for Depression	
	Risk for Depression
No Parent Depressed	10% for men 20% for women
One Parent Depressed	20% for men 40% for women
Identical Twin Depressed	50% for both sexes

Nature vs. Nurture

In the past, psychologists emphasized the role of environment, particularly a mother's influence, as the basis for depression. Presently, neuroscientists focus on genes and the biochemistry of nature. As it turns out, both nature and nurture are equally important causes for depression.

Identical twins start their lives with the exact same genes and basic programming for brain chemistry. Studies show that when one identical twin develops depression, the risk of his or her sibling developing the illness is 50 percent.[3] This is a far higher number than the 15-percent rate seen in the general population but far lower than the 100-percent rate expected if inherited genes were the only cause for depression. Clearly, depression is caused by both genetic and environmental events.

Looking at a Two-Hit Model

The interplay of genetic programming (nature) and environmental influences (nurture) in causing depression can be illustrated using a "two-hit" model, the same model used to understand the onset of most other illnesses. A genetic predisposition to develop chemical imbalance is the first hit. A subsequent alteration of brain chemistry by stress or exposure to toxins is the second hit. When combined, they trigger depression.

The first hit most often involves the inheritance of a defective gene predisposing a person to illness. The gene may have become defective in remote generations. However, the first hit does not cause illness unless combined with a second hit.

The second hit may occur anytime during a person's life span, such as when a pregnant mother develops a viral infection that passes to the child. Or the second hit may result from an excessive amount of work, leading to unhealthy amounts of stress and triggering the chemical cascade (see chapter 3). Second hits may occur when stress gets intense or lasts a long time. When the second hit occurs in someone already possessing a defective gene, depression may be triggered.

For now, this is the best understanding we have. In 20 years, these models of depression will be replaced. Old ways of understanding depression—or diabetes or cancer—will give way to new insights. As scientists discover the secrets of creation, they will begin to understand more fully the chemical balances that permit the healthy expression of emotion and hopefully discover more effective treatments for the breakdowns that lead to black moods.

Be Mindful of the Risk

Having a family history of any illness should alert you to your own risk of developing the same affliction. For women with a family history of breast cancer, the importance of regular mammograms is clear. For men with a history of prostate cancer in the family, the need for careful monitoring should also be clear. Similar concepts of early recognition and treatment should apply to those with a family history of black moods.

Unfortunately, many families hide or deny depression. Parents may be embarrassed to admit that Aunt Susie or Uncle Joe had a problem with it. This lack of awareness leads to delays in treatment.

Family denial

Alan, a 40-year-old financial advisor, had become estranged from his wife and children and was unable to work. He came to my office after assaulting his wife's new boyfriend with a knife.

When I asked if anyone in his family had suffered with depression, he said no. But he had seven brothers and sisters and just as many aunts and uncles. This was a very large family, and it was highly unlikely that no one had ever suffered from black moods. In his family, as it turned out, the illness was seen as a sign of personal weakness. Denial of depression in the family and ignoring the symptoms led to relationship problems and unnecessary suffering for Alan.

He's responding well to counseling and re-establishing relationships with his children. He won't ignore signs of depression if they show up in his children, nor will he hide the family history of black moods.

For parents with depression, it makes sense to keep a watchful eye on the mood changes of your children—not to overreact to normal moody moments, but to recognize a pattern of chronic sadness or irritability. If questions arise about "normal" or "not normal," refer to a description of depressive symptoms like the one at the end of this book. If problems with mood are interfering with performance at school, work, or friendships, then think about getting a professional opinion.

If your parents suffer with depression, stress management is more important for you than it might be for others. Making healthy choices will reduce the impact of environmental stress on your brain. Read the SMART Steps for recovery with an eye to prevention. If you respond rightly to stressful situations, you will lessen your risk for black moods.

Key Points

- Genetic inheritance accounts for about half of the risk factors for developing depression. Environmental influences are responsible for the other 50 percent.

- Genes for building the serotonin transporter are defective in some people with depression. Pieces of material are missing on the shorter form of this gene.

- Children of parents with depressive illness have twice the risk of developing the problem as children of parents without the illness.

- Lowering stress levels for ourselves and our children will reduce the likelihood of developing depressive illness.

- A family history of depression, like history of heart disease, should prompt careful attention to signs of difficulty and early treatment if necessary.

Chapter 6
Unmet Emotional Needs

*"Fathers, do not embitter your children, or they
will become discouraged."*

COLOSSIANS 3:21

Blaming your parents is the wrong way to deal with depression, but ignoring their roles in emotional development can be equally wrong. The ideas presented in this chapter aren't intended to inflame your anger over past injustices. That would only aggravate your sense of injury and cause more problems for present-day relationships. Instead, this chapter is intended to help you recognize the roots of depression in your childhood experience and to encourage you to dig them out. It will challenge you to change the way you respond to memories of childhood events.

In my counseling of people in black moods, three unmet needs of childhood keep coming up. These core emotional needs are to feel *generally safe, basically good, and powerful enough to make changes in the world.* When these three needs are met in childhood, people usually adjust pretty well to hardships as adults. When these needs go unmet, people often become depressed as adults. Lasting recovery may require a change in the way they think about these needs.

When core needs are not met, children may develop unhealthy patterns of responding to life's challenges. Some give up too easily.

In difficult challenges they resign themselves too quickly because of unmet core needs. (I call these *childhood resignations*.) Others try too hard, overcompensating in their attempts to meet basic needs. (I call these *childhood vows*.) These patterns of giving up too easily or trying too hard may lead to unhealthy stress-hormone responses and the chemical cascade. As we have seen, delicate brain-cell branches can then be damaged, leading to mood-messenger misfire and depression.

Core Emotional Needs

- Feeling of *safety*
- Belief in yourself as a *good* person
- Sense of *power* to change the world

By developing healthier responses to unmet core needs, adults can experience emotional and physical healing. Satisfying core needs by adjusting expectations will lower stress levels and allow the brain's natural healing process to take over.

Core Need #1: Feeling Safe

The most basic emotional need of children and adults is to feel safe in the world. When parents teach children to feel emotionally and physically safe, they build a platform for them to feel secure as adults. On the other hand, when life lessons teach children that they must remain on constant guard against threats to their safety, they grow up with gnawing insecurities.

Not-safe resignations. Ann came to my office consumed with fear. She was convinced that something dreadful was going to happen to her family at any moment. Fear circled around in her mind day after day. Her lips trembled, and her voice cracked. Her husband did most of the talking. She couldn't focus her mind on my questions. Fear had become her way of life.

She agreed to try counseling and medication, mostly to please her husband and two teenage sons. Counseling was slow. She felt oddly uneasy about letting down her guard, and she didn't like digging up the roots of her fears.

We talked about early days in her family. Her mother had also struggled with dark moods. Her father drank too much and lost his temper quite often. The family lived in a bowl of emotionally soured soup. Mother criticized daughter for not making her happy. Father yelled at daughter for making mother angry. Ann couldn't escape the verbal attacks. She would retreat to her room and hide in the closet. Her father would find her and call her out of her safe place. Eventually, she stopped even trying to find a safe place to hide.

Though Ann longed to be safe, she was equally fearful of silence. Quietness became as scary as conflict because each peaceful moment would soon be followed by abuse. She learned to keep silent and not wish for anything, resigning herself to the belief she would never be safe.

Ann's sense of living in danger increased in her thirties. Her mother killed herself by hanging. This amplified Ann's fears of losing her new family. With a trembling voice she informed me, "Something bad is going to happen to my husband." I attempted to comfort her with the fact that her husband was sitting beside her and appeared to be doing quite well.

As if not hearing my words, she dismissed my support. Relaxing her worrying would only bring trouble. She remained helplessly resigned to the false beliefs that her world was unsafe and there was nothing anyone could do to change it. Almost pleading, she expressed the wish to return to the home of her childhood, reasoning that actual old pain would be better than the fear of unpredictable new pain.

With treatment and time, Ann began to feel better. In therapy, she learned to confront false beliefs about her safety. She began to replace childhood fears with adult viewpoints of security and contentment. Still shy, but showing growing confidence, she began to come to appointments with a smile on her face. She would have good things to report about her family and friends. But even these good feelings became a source of concern. She was convinced she didn't deserve to feel better and would probably live to regret it.

She asked for permission to stop her medication and counseling and return to the way it was before. Her husband said no. Her doctor said no. For brief periods, she appears to understand that the world is usually quite safe. Still, in private quiet moments she often returns to her old thoughts that the world isn't safe and there's nothing she can do to change it. It simply takes time to overcome deeply ingrained childhood resignations.

Childhood Resignations and Vows

1. Resigning too easily:
   a. "I cannot be *safe*."
   b. "I'm not *good* enough."
2. Overcompensating vows:
   a. "I will not be hurt again."
   b. "Others must recognize my goodness."

Vows to gain safety. Others respond to fears of childhood by making a vow to create a safe world for themselves and their loved ones. It's a noble ambition to help others to avoid pain and feel secure. The vow is healthy when made within reason. A child who is treated poorly by his parents may vow to become a better parent himself. The next generation's parents and children will benefit from this childhood vow. However, when vows can't be attained or are inflexible, they become sources for frustration, high stress, and black moods.

Barbara responded to her childhood fears by vowing to make the world safe for others. She became the first woman to join the county's ambulance squad. She thrived as an intensive-care nurse and protector of her loved ones. She made these accomplishments without understanding the roots of her motivation. She had blocked out her memories of childhood abuse and her vow to keep others safe.

She came to my office a few weeks after the September 11 attacks in New York and Washington, DC. This rescue worker and ICU nurse was strangely overwhelmed by the disaster. She couldn't sleep. She woke up at night with feelings of panic, pacing and shaking for no reason. Uncontrolled worry carried her into depression.

As most counselors do, I encouraged her to talk about recent events and those of her childhood. Nothing remarkable came out. She spoke proudly of her father, an officer in the army, and her beautiful socialite mother. She seemed to be getting better with time and supportive counseling.

Three months later, her granddaughter started menstruation. Thoughts of the bleeding triggered Barbara to recall her own repressed memories of bleeding. Anxieties overwhelmed her. She began crying uncontrollably and passed out on the floor. She was reliving the memories of her father's sexual abuse.

Several more weeks of counseling passed. Barbara opened up about the pain of her childhood and its impact on her present relationships. We began talking about her pattern of overreacting to minor problems. A childhood vow to make the world safe became clear.

Barbara's hidden vow to make the world safe was most evident in her home. She married a policeman. Without knowing the source of her fears, he recognized her desperate need to feel safe. He installed double locks on the doors and a motion-sensor alarm system in each room of the house. His efforts to satisfy her overarching need for safety did not end her fears.

Driven by her need to protect, she continued to worry about the safety of her family and friends. Their everyday hardships triggered feelings of fright. If one of them was late to dinner or didn't answer the phone this started the wheels of worry in motion. Her excessive responses to arguments and illnesses provided evidence of her over-compensating need to protect. With tortured empathy, she felt the distress of loved ones and labored to relieve them of suffering. Some people really do care too much.

As therapy proceeded, we explored the source of her excessive worry. Between the ages of 9 and 16, Barbara had been sexually abused by her father. Her mother had failed to stop it. Barbara vowed to become the opposite of her mother—the "anti-mom" of her childhood, the vigilant guardian of her loved ones. But this noble goal was unrealistic and nearly led to her demise. She cried every day, lost 40 pounds, and spent evenings wishing to be dead. She was angry with God for not protecting her loved ones.

Barbara is not giving up on counseling. She's learning to disconnect her childhood fears from present-day challenges, to feel safe and let go of her unreasonable vow. She knows, but still struggles with the idea, that she cannot protect all loved ones from all pain. The fear that rests in the back of her mind is resolving itself as she puts words to the pain of her past and rethinks events of the present. As a middle-aged adult she's learning the most basic childhood belief—she is safe.

Core Need #2: Believing You're a Good Person

Believing you're a basically good person refers to how you see yourself in regard to your family and community—the feeling that you belong and have value to others. Satisfying this second core need enables the child and adult to stand strong in the midst of criticism.

Children learn this belief from their parents. They internalize parents' teachings about self-worth in their unconscious memories. This "internalized parent" speaks to the child from the earliest years of life until the last breaths. The child either hears the encouraging message "You're a good person," or the discouraging one "You're not good enough." If the voice of her mother, in her memory, tells her, "You're a good person," then she'll expect others to feel the same way and treat her with respect. If her internal mom says, "You're not a good person" or "I wish you were gone," she'll expect her friends on the bus to brush her aside.

Simply stated, it's a message we all learn: you're a good person—or not. If your need to feel like a basically good person is satisfied, you will defy the opinion of your third-grade teacher who says you're too slow. You'll dispute the criticism of your volleyball coach who says you have no talent. Why? You got the basic message "I am a good person—and if you don't believe me then go ask my mom."

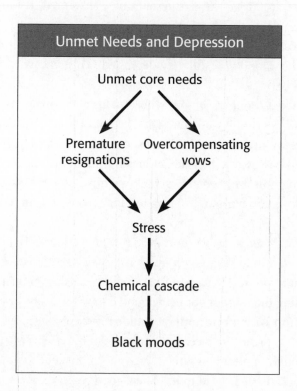

Unmet Needs and Depression

Unmet core needs

Premature resignations   Overcompensating vows

Stress

Chemical cascade

Black moods

Vows to prove goodness. Most of us struggle with feelings of not being good enough in some area of our lives. These struggles can lead to remarkable accomplishments in people who passionately seek to demonstrate their value. But trying too hard to meet this basic need may lead to black moods.

Jim came to my office after his discharge from the hospital. He had been treated for severe depression with psychotic thinking. Unmanageable stress had led to sleepless nights, depression, and delusions. In the midst of black moods, Jim had developed the belief that he could communicate with computers. The computers, he believed, were sending him messages warning about the impending destruction of the world. He was arrested after trying to pull a woman from her car while waiting in line at a drive-through restaurant. He wanted to warn her of impending doom.

Medical treatment in the hospital helped to clear up Jim's thinking, but his mood was still very depressed. This was when he came to my office.

We talked about his job, his wife, and his emotional struggles. He took a few months off work to rest and begin counseling for depression. The excessive drive for professional success appeared to be his source of present-day distress. He had graduated from one of the nation's best MBA programs and become a chief executive officer by age 30. He was working too hard and resting too little, so we began looking for reasons why he couldn't relax.

We uncovered a sorely unmet need rooted in childhood. Jim's father had pushed him to success through harsh criticism. Perfection was the only right response. Other performance was punished or belittled. His most telling memory of not being good enough was one of his father beating him with a belt until he couldn't move his legs, for refusing to complete piano practice. Jim can't remember a day when he was good enough to please his father. Even enormous professional success could not satisfy his need to feel like a good person.

In an era of maximizing worker productivity, it may seem odd to encourage someone to shoot for mediocrity, but this was what Jim needed. He's now learning to accept average as good enough. He recognizes the tendency to revive his childhood vow, but is learning to say no to blind ambition. Releasing himself from his unreachable vow to always do better feels strange and uncomfortable—but freeing. Today, he produces educational software, not to prove his own goodness, but to help others succeed.

Jim has a wife who loves him as he is. She does not require great success or perfection. Jim is *good*. If you don't believe him, then go ask his wife. She understands his struggle and is helping him be happy with himself as he is. Sometimes core needs can be satisfied within healthy new relationships.

Core Need #3: Having a Sense of Power to Change Your Environment

A sense of power to make changes in the world is the third core emotional need. When this need is satisfied in childhood, adults gain confidence, whether to go to the store or climb a mountain. Some parents teach children how to exercise power in healthy ways and to face failures as temporary setbacks.

Other parents teach children to give up too early. Perhaps unintentionally, they teach them an attitude of helplessness. Excessive restrictions teach children to relinquish their power to change the world.

Even the anger that follows restriction may be punished too severely. When children are denied the reasonable expression of the emotions that follow restrictions, they may have difficulty managing their emotions as adults. Bottled-up feelings of anger and regret will lead to emotional confusion. The child doesn't know what to do or what to feel next. Frustrating life events become sources of festering anger that lead to black moods.

Power deficits. Mary's mother believed she was doing the right things. She was teaching discipline and protecting her daughter from the dangerous world. However, she went too far. Day after day, she taught her daughter that she was helpless to make choices and that the world outside must be avoided.

To Mary, home began to feel like a prison. Her friends were unwelcome because playing caused too much mess. Any signs of standing up for herself resulted in Mary's being sent to her room. In her room, Mary's sense of power was further erased as she was punished for showing signs of disappointment. She was not allowed to explore her neighborhood, her home, or her own emotions.

As an adult, Mary feels powerless. The slight rudeness and disrespect everyone faces while shopping is experienced as overwhelming intimidation by Mary. She rarely goes out. Overwhelming fear and anger meet her when she does. She never learned to feel the power to alter her world, and she has remained clinically depressed for most of her life.

In therapy, she's recognizing the false teachings of early life and using logic to confront false beliefs about herself. Her childhood beliefs about her helplessness are changing. She's finding courage to go shopping and attend her son's school events—big steps of relearning basic truths about power.

As a parent herself, Mary is teaching power to her son. She fosters his confidence in his ability to change the world. He has parties, has friends over, messes up the house, and freely expresses the emotions of a normal adolescent. She has some trouble teaching discipline—it reminds her too much of her mother. But her husband helps with this. Mary may not be able to fully undo the false teachings of her childhood, but she's succeeding in efforts to help her son find satisfaction of his basic emotional needs.

Progress, Not Perfection

Satisfying core needs is a process. Eighteen years of childhood experience can't be undone with a few weeks of counseling or grit-your-teeth determination. When parents and life experiences teach children to feel unsafe, not good enough, or too weak to change things, it takes time to unlearn these false ideas.

Counseling can help change patterns of overreacting or resigning to threats and promote satisfaction of emotional needs. Satisfying one of these needs will empower you to satisfy the other two, moving you closer to the mind that God intends you to possess.

Next-generation families can help. A supportive spouse or loving child can provide opportunities to satisfy needs not met in childhood. A middle-aged mom recently told me, "I'm not the bad seed I once thought I was. My husband doesn't treat me like that!"

Spiritual devotion and supportive communities also help. The Scriptures can open your eyes so you can see yourself as God does— forgivable and perfectly acceptable in His eyes. Healthy church families offer nurturing relationships that may serve as models for new ways of relationship.

Sometimes medication is needed. The fears and hurts of unmet core needs can produce unhealthy levels of stress hormones and brain injury. Antidepressants help control stress responses and raise growth-factor levels, facilitating the healing of brain cells and making counseling and self-examination more effective.

Just as depressive illness can become more and more destructive over time, recovery can lead to more and more healing of body, mind, and spirit. Healing of emotions promotes recovery of the brain, and the mending of brain cells restores mental processing. In a similar way, emotional resilience and spiritual vitality are interdependent, invigorating each other in a process of renewal.

Chapters 15 and 16 will keep this process going as we look deeper into the role of satisfying basic needs and revising relationships. Deeply felt healing of emotions must include forgiveness of the ones who have hurt us in the past.

Key Points

- Healthy parents teach children to feel safe, good, and powerful enough to make some changes in the world.
- Meeting core needs reduces stress and the risk of black moods.
- Counseling, spirituality, and medication may each have a role in the process of satisfying core needs.
- Satisfying one core need helps to satisfy each of the others.

For example, feeling good about yourself promotes feelings of safety and power.

- God created man to feel safe, know his value, and exercise power in the world. He provides ways to grow in healthy self-esteem.

Chapter 7

Repression and the Unconscious

When physical injuries occur, they leave a bruise or some other reminder of the event. The same is true of mental injuries. When emotionally painful things happen, they leave a mark. Sometimes the memory mark is conscious, and other times it's blocked from awareness in the unconscious.

As you think back on childhood events, you'll probably recall painful or deeply affecting moments that shaped your thinking and guided your choices. Yet many events you won't recall—some forgotten, others deeply hidden in unconscious memory. Experiences that shaped your feelings of safety, being a good person, and having the power to change your surroundings are stored in both conscious memories and unconscious memory compartments. To gain a fuller understanding of the satisfaction of core emotional needs, which we discussed in the previous chapter, we must consider unconscious levels of the mind.

In contemporary terms, unconscious memory is like the software that runs a computer (the operating system). Behind the display screen are millions of coded messages that tell the system what to do next. The computer cannot process information contrary to its basic programming. If it contains faulty information, the system functions poorly. For the human brain, parents and caretakers do the basic programming. If, when you were 2 years old, 10 years old, and 12 years old, your parents taught you that you were a good child, you believed it. If, on the other hand, when you were 2, 10, and 12 they taught you that you were worthless, you probably believed that. When core beliefs are "installed" incorrectly, mental systems malfunction. If these programming errors are unconscious, they must be made conscious in order to be recognized and corrected. *Psychodynamic psychotherapy* aims to uncover and revise unconscious memory.

Insight from Sigmund Freud

Freud's insights into how forgotten childhood events continue to influence adult behavior revolutionized psychodynamic psychology. Appreciating his theories is indispensable to understanding how experiences of the past guide behavior of the present. Acceptance of Freud's theories, however, has been slow in Christian circles due to his injection of atheistic beliefs into psychological teaching.[1] His rejection of spirituality and his excessive focus on childhood sexuality detract from an otherwise marvelous model of the mind.

As with all learning, we benefit by accepting statements that we judge to be true and rejecting those we discern to be false. We may benefit from theories of the unconscious as we separate psychological wisdom from Freud's spiritual ignorance. C.S. Lewis described the need to make this distinction in the following way:

> Psychoanalysis itself, apart from all the philosophical additions that Freud and others have made to it, is not in the least contradictory to Christianity. Its teaching overlaps with Christian morality at some points and it would not be a bad thing if every person knew something about it.[2]

Freud's most basic theory of the mind is summarized in his *topographical model*, a depiction of personal awareness that categorizes levels of awareness into *conscious, preconscious,* and *unconscious.* Unconscious memories are unavailable for recall under most circumstances. They appear to be forgotten, yet they quietly direct our behavior without our being aware of it. Memories too painful to remember are repressed in the unconscious to prevent further emotional suffering. Although this theory has been controversial, it's finding new support as experiments show that people actually can block out unwanted memories as a way of minimizing their negative effects.[3]

Freud's second major theory of the unconscious is illustrated in his *structural model.* Here he develops the concepts of *ego, id,* and *superego* to explain the mechanisms of motivation. Biological drives for sex and aggression are contained in the id, and the moral teachings of society are parts of the superego. The id and superego are partly conscious and partly unconscious. In this model, the ego is the conscious awareness of everyday life, the mediator between self-centered urges of the id and moral restraint of the superego. According to Freud, anxiety and depression result from collision between the urges of the id and the restraints of the superego.

Christian Insights

Much of Freud's structural model overlaps with the Christian understanding of motivation as described by the apostle Paul. Similar to Freud's discussion of conflicts between superego and id, Paul described struggles between spirit and flesh (many hundreds of years earlier):

> I find this law at work: When I want to do good, evil is right there with me. For in my inner being I delight in God's law; but I see another law at work in the members of my body, waging war against the law of my mind and making me a prisoner of the law of sin at work within my members (Romans 7:21-25).

In the structural model, we are driven by appetites of the id and restrained by the influence of the superego, a conflict remarkably similar to Paul's description of struggle between the temptations of the body and the desire for righteousness.

Freud's description departs from Paul's by dismissing spiritual sources. In his quest to uncover deeper motivations, Freud overlooked humanity's deepest need—a desire to commune with our creator. Yes,

right and wrong moral choices are motivated by teachings of parents
and may be incorporated into a superego concept—but the Spirit also
guides choices between right and wrong. The Holy Spirit prompts us
to righteousness, while the temptations of the body spring from and
lead to self-indulgence. Freud's narrow focus misses these important
influences on behavior. Both moral teachings and supernatural communion combine to influence choices between right and wrong and
motivate behavior.

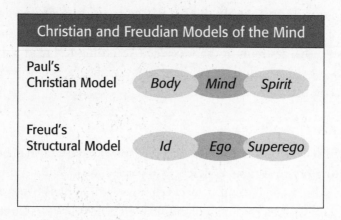

A holistic perspective of the unconscious mind incorporates the role
of the Holy Spirit. Many Christians experience conscious prompting
of the Spirit, urging them to conform their behavior to God's will.
Others also recognize that the Holy Spirit empowers their minds unconsciously, enabling them to speak with words of wisdom or perform acts
of sacrifice beyond their natural abilities. Without their awareness of
how it occurs, the spirit of God quietly expresses righteous words and
behavior through their lives—another marvelous mystery of unconscious motivation.

Memory Repression

In homes of abuse or neglect some lessons were too painful to remember. These were moved from conscious to unconscious compartments.

Silently, in the background, unconscious memories guard behavior to prevent repetition of behaviors that seemed to cause pain in the past. Memory of childhood abuse, for example, may be blocked from awareness (repressed), yet quietly warn the adult to remain watchful for similar threats. Sexual abuse is arguably the most disturbing form of child abuse—love and pain and hate get mixed together in memories too hurtful to reconcile. Such repressed memories are some of the most powerful unconscious motivators of behavior.

Needs for safety and feeling good about oneself are completely frustrated in the betraying act of abuse. Memories are often stuffed away, locked in the unconscious as a way of making life feel safe. When they resurface, memories of trauma are disturbing to the calm, unaware mind. Opening the door to repressed memories leads to escalating fears that the world is unsafe, then to feelings of helpless depression.

Robyn's experience of the reemergence of repressed memory. During a visit to her gynecologist's office for an endometrial biopsy, Robyn's mind became flooded with anxiety and confusion. She punched the nurse and shouted obscenities at the doctor. For years she had completely repressed memories of childhood sexual abuse; she had discussed the events with no one. Twenty years later, under the stress of a minor surgical procedure and the pressure of her upcoming wedding, repressed memories resurfaced.

Psychoanalyzing her experience in terms of unmet core needs shows how repression works. For Robyn, her id is the memory compartment holding unconscious memories and feelings of fear and anger. Her superego is the compartment for stored moral teachings of parents— what it means to be a good girl. Sexual abuse robbed her of satisfying the core need to feel safe. The abuse incited rage (id) and confused her sense of right and wrong (superego). This id–superego conflict was too much. Rather than tremble helplessly in the corner, she reflexively repressed the memory. Like a reflex hammer to the knee, sexual trauma triggered automatic repression of the memory. Repression is a built-in survival reflex that allowed Robyn to deny fear and anger and consider herself to be safe, good, and powerful. By repressing these memories, she could act as if core needs had actually been met. For many years, she was able to consider herself safe and quite a good person.

Through her teen years and early adult life, she performed very well, unaware of her traumatic past. As her wedding approached, sexual feelings made her uneasy. She began to feel unexplainably angry toward her father. When a painful medical exam triggered recall of past pelvic pain, she reacted as if the childhood trauma were occurring right then. Rage bottled up in her id burst into her awareness as she hit the nurse in the face and screamed obscenities at the doctor. For one brief moment, the doctor became the image of her abusive father and the nurse, the image of her passive mother. Superego teachings that good girls must not fight their fathers came crashing into her awareness, and guilt overwhelmed her. Id urges and superego teachings were in conflict. Intense fear and anger led to depression.

In the weeks that followed, she talked about childhood events as if they had happened yesterday. Her words were full of emotion, revealing the anger and shame of someone who had just been raped. She grieved the loss of her innocence and the esteem she'd had for her father. Release of unconscious memories gave her a real opportunity to address her unmet needs for sense of safety, goodness, and power. With rest, medication, and careful reflection on the false teachings of her father, Robyn was able to return to work and get married. In years that followed, she revisited the issues of safety and self-worth in light of this "new" experience.

Most people will not experience stress to this level and will not completely repress bad memories. Even so, we possess partially forgotten childhood memories that alter our behavior. Milder mistreatment that led to resentment of their parents may cause some people to overreact to authority figures. Repressed anger toward a father may be displaced on a present-day husband. Past safety violations and criticisms rest invisibly in your unconscious, influencing your opinion of yourself and your place in the world.

Opening the Box

Sometimes it's necessary to open the box; other times it's better to leave the box of memories sealed up in the unconscious. Or, as in Robyn's situation, the box can pop open under times of stress. Choosing whether or not to explore repressed memories is a complicated decision, and it may be best handled in a relationship with a supportive counselor.

When repressed memories create unexplained anxiety and sleeping problems that interfere with your ability to work or engage in healthy relationships, it's usually necessary to open the box. In times like these, allowing yourself to remember past traumas can become a first step to healing, through reprocessing old events. Discussing past traumas can soften the feelings of fear, helplessness, and shame that often accompany trauma in early life.

For many people, coaxing forgotten memories to the surface can be done with a series of simple questions such as "What was your most fearful moment in childhood?" For others, more time and support, and a more delicate approach, are needed. Disclosing such embarrassing memories requires an environment of trust and a recognized need to be open and honest.

When undergoing counseling about past trauma, it may not be necessary to completely unpack memories of the past. Quite often, it can be helpful to simply acknowledge a few of the bad things, understand those events in a adult frame of mind, and move on to discuss better ways of handling stressful events of today.

ഇരുള

We all have bad experiences from the past that we would rather forget. And for most of us leaving past problems in the past is the best idea. However, there's also a right time and right way to reopen the box of repressed memories. These sources of excessive worry and depression can often be uprooted in counseling, leading to freedom of emotional expression and healthier relationships with loved ones today.

Key Points

1. Memories of the past may be stored in the unconscious... apparently forgotten.

2. Unconscious memories can motivate behavior today.

3. A holistic understanding of motivation includes both spiritual and natural ways of describing the subliminal functions of the mind. (*Subliminal* means "existing or functioning below the level of consciousness.")

4. The apostle Paul provides a spiritual perspective on the struggle between subconscious self-serving drives and healthier spiritual aspirations.

5. Sigmund Freud described a similar struggle between the unconscious drives of the self-serving id and moral superego. Freud's atheistic blindness should not diminish our opinion of the insight to be gained through his study of the unconscious.

6. Unconscious struggles can resurface under stress, becoming sources for depression.

7. For people who experienced traumatic events in childhood, healing of depression may require recovery and reprocessing of unconscious memory.

Chapter 8

Problems of Spiritual Personality

*"Why are you so downcast, O my soul? Why so
disturbed within me?"*

PSALM 42:11

We all have particular personalities. Just think about your family and friends. Their unique characters shape the ways they get along with others during a football game, small-group meeting, or holiday dinner. Uncle Joe is so quiet and withdrawn that he's too timid to ask someone to pass the cucumbers. Aunt Louise is so loud and self-centered that she dominates the conversation with her stories of bunions and cataracts.

Psychiatrists consider personality disorders to be longstanding maladaptive (badly adapted) ways of interacting with others. This pattern of behavior develops in adolescence and influences the way we think about ourselves and relate to other people. Personality problems hamper the growth of intimacy in relationships and lead to distress in the person with the disorder.

Our "spiritual personalities" can also become disordered, hampering our relationship with God and the communion we experience with Him. Our spiritual personality will determine our viewpoint on religious and moral concerns, such as guilt and forgiveness. It may cause emotional anguish and diminish the closeness we develop with God.

Six spiritual personality problems are described in this chapter. These longstanding maladaptive ways of relating to God may contribute to depression. They can also be changed through self-examination, counseling, and spiritual experience.

Problems of Spiritual Personality

- Spiritually estranged
- Morally callous
- Guilt-gripped
- Faith-impaired
- Church-injured
- Evil-obsessed

Spiritual Estrangement

The first problem that can affect our spiritual personality is being spiritually estranged. Atheists, agnostics, materialists, and humanists are clearly alienated from their Creator—spiritually unaware—incapable of developing a relationship with someone they choose to ignore.

To become the person God created you to be, you must know who He is. Blindness to eternal purpose leaves many good people feeling lost in existential anxiety. They want to know "What am I doing here?" "What is it all for?" They have a God-sized hole in their souls, a need for purpose and perspective in life.

Being reborn spiritually opens the mind's eye to the goodness of God and spiritual pathways to healing. While knowing God does not prevent black moods, research shows that religious belief lowers the risk.[1] People who participate in religious activities have fewer thoughts of suicide and fewer suicide attempts.[2] Religious belief satisfies our spiritual hunger. It satisfies the hard-to-describe sense that something is missing.

God created this spiritual hunger. He can satisfy it. Jesus said, "I am the bread of life. He who comes to me will never go hungry" (John 6:35). Getting right with Him satisfies that hard-to-define spiritual craving. Without Him, people look to other sources.

Roberto's story. A troubled young businessman came to my office for help. Despite the blessings of a beautiful family and thriving small business, he was depressed. Previous counseling had not worked. Anti-depressant medications were not helping. When I asked him about his spiritual beliefs, he described himself as an atheist. His brother and parents were believers. He wasn't interested.

Without a spiritual ideal or religious commitment, Roberto drifted to material sources of enjoyment. He looked for pleasure and purpose in more money, more sex, and more drugs. In time, they all became pointless. After long days at work, he would return home feeling like his existence was meaningless.

Our conversation returned to spirituality. I asked him, "How do atheists do it?"

"We use drugs," he glibly replied.

His words reflected his dry sense of humor as well as his frustration with life. Clearly, not all atheists use drugs. Many live emotionally balanced lives without substance abuse. Without a spiritual compass, they seek their own way. Roberto was also committed to finding his own way.

One afternoon, after a binge on cocaine, he returned to my office—disheveled, despondent, and at the end of himself. He was sick about what he was making of his life (a good time to reach out to God). He humbled himself enough to wonder out loud, "Is God real?"

Nothing else had worked, so he awkwardly asked me how to believe. We talked about the message of Christianity. He had heard it many times before, but now he was ready to listen. He prayed for forgiveness and opened his heart to God, then waited. A broad smile took the place of worried despair. Then, with a sheepish expression on his face, he asked me, "Well, what's next?" We talked about meeting with other Christians and how to make progress. Roberto's spiritual rebirth marked a turning point in his recovery from depression. He asked for guidance from a pastor friend he had known for some time. Golf became for him fun again. Work again became a stimulating way to pass the day.

Not all spiritual rebirths will end the illness of dark moods. Not all atheists will get depressed, nor will all Christians avoid depression. Even so, the most important step for Roberto in breaking through depression was gaining a spiritual vision.

Moral Callousness

In personal relationships, callousness leads to insensitivity about the feelings and interests of other people. It leads to conflicts with family and friends and increases the likelihood of depression. In spiritual relationships, callousness leads to disregard of God's desire for friendship with us and disrespect for what He says. Spiritual callousness leads to self-serving behaviors and disregard for the destructiveness of wrongdoing.

There are at least two unhelpful ways to think about wrongdoing: 1) It's possible for a person to completely refrain from it. 2) It doesn't matter, because everything will be forgiven anyway. Both of these beliefs puff us up with pride and stop us from looking for help. Even more serious, they block us from relating to God. He is the only one who can give us the spiritual help we need.

Our Creator did not make us in such a way that we could live with significance apart from Him. He has done everything needed to allow us to relate to Him. He forgives our wrongdoing because His Son, Jesus, died for it. It does not matter what we have done.

God's generosity with forgiveness is hard to understand. He is more patient with us than appears to make sense. He has made it simple for us to turn to Him. We can ignore His friendship by remaining self-focused and continuing to do wrong. Then we will never receive the help we need. And we will probably suffer the natural consequences of our wrong actions.

As an example, Solomon describes the physical and mental problems that often follow drunkenness: "Who has bloodshot eyes? Those who linger over wine...Your eyes will see strange sights and your mind imagine confusing things" (Proverbs 23:29-30,33). Continued alcohol abuse may lead to depression, cirrhosis of the liver, and death. Sexual wrongdoing may also bring sickness and ruin. Solomon writes, "The lips of an adulteress drip honey...but in the end...her feet go down to death" (Proverbs 5:3-5). Taking wrong sexual actions lightly may lead to HIV infection, divorce, and death.

We make it easier to ignore our wrongdoing if we describe the behaviors in nicer-sounding terms. "Adult entertainment" replaces lust. "Recreational drug use" replaces substance abuse. "Casual affairs" takes the place of adultery, and "alternative lifestyles" takes the place of homosexual acting out. The list of "not-so-bad" wrong things is a long one. Look deep enough and you'll find one of your own. Disregarding these "not so bad" wrong actions increases the risk of depression and becomes a longstanding maladaptive trait that stands in the way of your relationship with God.

Owning up to our wrongdoing and releasing our rights to pursue selfish goals diminishes our spiritual callousness, awakening a new spiritual sensitivity to God, who can help us. Still, we may suffer from depressed moods, a natural consequence of unhealthy choices.

The Grip of Guilt

A wise older woman complained to me that pastors don't "preach people under conviction" anymore. She was talking about preaching that calls sin what it is and urges people to turn their lives around. She recognized that this can be a tool to help people with the ongoing cleanup of their lives. A wise younger woman also taught me that too much focus on wrong actions creates unhealthy guilt and shame.

Healthy development of spiritual personality balances an inner pressure to do right with the awareness that God has given us the gift of forgiveness. Good guilt includes a joyful appreciation of forgiveness as well as a painful awareness of the awfulness and damage of wrongdoing. Guilt is healthy when directed by the Spirit of God. It is not healthy when it comes from a habit of finding fault with yourself despite prayers for forgiveness and change in behavior.

Thoughts and prompts from the Holy Spirit produce a healthy struggle that is intended to bring change of mind, forgiveness, and surrender. Christians are at their best when fully surrendered to God—in a sense, unconcerned about wrong actions. Yet often we struggle with what we know to be right. Although it is better to surrender than struggle, even a period of spiritual strife can facilitate growth. As we reach toward right living and battle with wrongdoing, we grow.

When you struggle with the memory of your past wrongs and do not apply forgiveness, guilt becomes a sickness, interfering with living the life that the Creator has in mind for you. While self-criticism serves to motivate right choices, obsession with wrongdoing leads to black moods.

Sometimes this sickness of guilt can be caused by a chemical imbalance in serotonin. Obsessive compulsive disorder (OCD) is an example of a serotonin imbalance that causes unreasonable self-blame. The obsession over guilt that comes with OCD may be controlled or stopped with the right medication.

Obsessive self-blame can also be taught. Most parents teach children to respect older people. Most church leaders teach members of their congregation to honor God. Each of these principles helps create healthy inner convictions...when criticism is applied in right measure.

Since honoring our parents is a biblical mandate, a measure of guilt is appropriate when we fail. However, some parents use this idea to create excessive guilt as a way to manipulate children. A mistaken sense of duty leads to frustration as the child is criticized for failing to meet unreasonable requests. Some people get stuck in dark moods because they dwell on these failures.

Freedom from guilt feelings

I know a woman who got stuck on guilty feelings related to not pleasing her mother. The hospital bed where her mother died marked the point of Tammy's last attempts to satisfy her mother's unreasonable demands. From four years old until forty, Tammy was incessantly criticized by her mother. From all I could tell, Tammy had been a loving, attentive, and self-sacrificing daughter. She could not let herself see things that way.

With the passing of her mother, any hope Tammy had of gaining her mother's respect also died. She was stuck in guilt and becoming deeply depressed. Assurances from her priest couldn't console her or convince her that God forgave her for perceived failures to honor her parents.

So she sought professional help. Medication helped lift her dark mood and ease her self-critical ways. Counseling helped her satisfy her core need to feel like a good person and accept forgiveness. She found a right balance between conviction and grace, and she learned to recognize that her behavior with her mother had been quite honorable. Freedom from obsessive guilt allowed her to enjoy a more vital spiritual life.

Impairment of Faith

Problems with faith are common to all believers. For example, the apostle Peter displayed this spiritual impairment at times. Consumed by fear at the time of Christ's crucifixion, he denied that Jesus was his friend—three times.

Earlier, in the middle of a lake, Peter saw Jesus walking toward him on the water. He asked Jesus if he could come out to meet Him.

> "Come," he said. Then Peter got down out of the boat, walked on the water and came toward Jesus. But when he saw the wind, he was afraid and, beginning to sink, cried out, "Lord, save me!" Immediately Jesus reached out his hand and caught him. "You of little faith," he said, "why did you doubt?" (Matthew 14:29-31).

Peter took his eyes off Jesus and started to worry about the waves. He focused on his problems and began to sink. Peter had no control of the waves. It was useless for him to consider the problem his own. Christ was there. Christ is here. He wants us to give our sense of responsibility for the waves to Him.

Ignoring the waves is made harder by black moods. Just as arthritis may impair your ability to move across the room, black moods make it hard to keep moving with faith. Brain cells malfunction. Problems appear magnified. Little ripples begin to look like overpowering surges.

The answer to worry is faithfulness. The spiritually reasonable thing to do, in the midst of life's challenges, is to give all your worries to God. It is self-centered to think that your worry is necessary or good. The Creator of the universe knows what He is doing, and He has promised to see you through any hard time.

> Do not be anxious about anything, but…present your requests to God. And the peace of God, which transcends all understanding, will guard your hearts and your minds in Christ Jesus (Philippians 4:6-7).

Paul says to settle down, ask for what you need, and trust. Rather than focus on yourself and your problems, keep your eyes on the Guide. He has not forgotten about you and will not let the waves pull you under if you remain focused on Him.

Development of spiritual personality takes time. Longstanding doubts are rarely overcome in a day. It took Peter many years of learning to develop a rock-solid faith…a faith that ended in his own crucifixion, demonstrating his belief that God is eternally in control.

Injury in Church

In the same way that early life experiences with our parents shape our personality, the influence of church leaders shapes our spiritual spirituality. Pastors, priests, elders, and other leaders have unique responsibilities in shaping the spiritual personalities of believers. Their job description includes the responsibility to point out wrong actions. If all goes well, this leads to good guilt, results in a change of mind, and ends with forgiveness. Forgiveness leads to freedom in our souls and spiritual restoration.

Nobody likes to be told something is wrong with him or her. It can be very disturbing for a doctor to tell you of a diagnosis, and it can be very unsettling to be challenged by a church leader about wrong-doing. Yet without the bad news, health-giving treatment cannot be offered, nor can forgiveness be gained.

Leaders, however, must be careful. Just as a surgeon uses a scalpel to inflict temporary pain in the process of healing, the spiritual leader may use guilt to cut away evil. And, just as surgeons sometimes cut the wrong part and cause injury, or cut the right part too deeply, pastors, priests, or elders may misapply guilt. Both errors leave scars and need help to heal.

One woman I have been seeing for several years was deeply injured by childhood church experiences. Her pastor's forceful and repetitive commands for repentance left her fearful and feeling helpless to please God. She repented and repented again. Each repentance was followed by another message that she was damned and must repent (again).

Week after week, year after year, her pastor evoked feelings of shame over unacknowledged wrongdoing. She was too afraid to sleep at night. Gradually, her prayers of repentance were replaced by the hopeless resignation to the belief that she would never find peace or forgiveness.

As a middle-aged woman, she will not go to church. When we talk about the subject, her eyes fill with fear, and her neck turns red with anger. She believes in God but doesn't believe in church. She refuses to return to the "houses of condemnation," where fear and shame threw her into depression. Medications have helped relieve her depression, and counseling has helped her face some of her fears, but scars of condemnation remain.

The Christian who expects perfection in word and deed in this world will always struggle. When Christ challenged His followers to "be perfect...as your heavenly Father is perfect" (Matthew 5:48), He was calling them to adopt a heartfelt goal to be different from the general public, not demanding moral perfection as a prerequisite for friendship with Him. Dare to be different—to be odd by the standards of popular culture—balancing the call to right living with a healthy awareness of God's mercy. No one but Christ is without sin—not pastors, priests, elders, evangelists, or nuns.

Obsession with Evil

The tendency to focus too much on Satan is another spiritual personality trait that may lead to black moods. Some people view illness as an attack from Satan. Others see it as something permitted by God for reasons beyond our understanding. The truth may rest somewhere between these views. C.S. Lewis described a balanced view of demons' influence in his preface to the famous *Screwtape Letters:*

> There are two equal and opposite errors into which our race can fall about devils. One is to disbelieve in their existence. The other is to believe, and to feel an excessive and unhealthy interest in them.[3]

To ignore satanic influence is to overlook Satan's deception in the Garden of Eden, the healings of Christ, and the power of the devil today. To feel an unhealthy interest in demons is to attribute to Satan power that isn't his. Christ is greater.

It's impossible to read and believe the Bible without acknowledging that Satan and his demons are real. Christ exorcised demons that caused illness. He healed an epileptic boy when He "rebuked an evil spirit" (Luke 9:37-42). He cured a man with severe depression by casting out demons:

> Night and day among the tombs and in the hills he would cry out and cut himself with stones...Jesus had said to him, "Come out of this man, you evil spirit"...And the evil spirits came out and went into the pigs (Mark 5:5,8,11).

The pigs ran down a hill, jumped in a lake, and died. In that day, God used exorcism to heal physical and mental illness, and to validate the truth of Christ's message.

Demonic possession or illness? Fifteen years ago, I treated a woman who appeared to be possessed. I met Sally in the middle of the night in a hospital's psychiatric unit. As I arrived on the floor, she was running at full speed toward the locked exit doors. She threw herself against them and fell to the floor. Running up behind her, nurses and orderlies tried to comfort her as she thrashed about on the floor. Once she was settled in bed, with her wrists and ankles restrained, I had my first opportunity to talk with her. I asked her how she was doing. She began screaming:

"I am going to kill the body!"

"I don't care if I break the wrists or not!"

"I am going to kill it!"

We gave Sally some sedating medication and time to settle down. She began to speak more clearly and attempted to explain that several persons were living inside her, including an angry adolescent boy who wanted to kill her.

Sexual abuse in childhood had left her traumatized. She remained depressed and confused. As a child, she had coped with experiences of abuse by imagining herself to be somebody else. This reflexive remaking of perceptions under stress is called *dissociation*. The fantasies helped her endure the abuse of childhood but left her mentally fragile as an adult. She was diagnosed with dissociative identity disorder (formerly called multiple personality disorder). Counseling addressed her sorely unmet need to feel safe. Medication lifted her mood and brought order to her thoughts. On that day, God used counselors and physicians to heal.

Focus on the One who is greater. In my practice, I've treated many people who looked like, sounded like, and behaved like they were possessed by demons. Most had already sought help from pastors, Christian counselors, or healing services at their churches. One young man was convinced he saw the glaring red eyes of Satan; another was tormented by Lucifer's voice. One depressed wife was convinced that her husband was conspiring against her using witchcraft. It is hard to say how many of these experiences were spiritually based and how many were physically based. It is easy to say that all of them got better with medication, counseling, and prayer.

By emphasizing the medical aspects of psychotic depression, I don't mean to say that evil spirits do not take over people's wills, only that I have not seen it. Pastors and psychiatrists I deeply respect have described to me how they have been used in demonic deliverance. The long-term recovery of these people who have been delivered from demons makes it hard to explain their responses in psychiatric terms.

Whether or not demon possession occurs today, it should not be a serious concern to believers. The power of Satan to overcome Christians is very doubtful. The Holy Spirit is greater. Rather than living in fear of Satan and becoming anxious and depressed, we would do better to get close to God so the devil won't be able to get near. This way of thinking often changes the focus of my patients who live in fear of the influence of demons.

Reshaping Your Spiritual Personality

Your goals for breaking through depression should not be limited to freedom from tears, cranky moods, or obsessive worries. Spiritual vitality that leads to new awareness of God's love and that empowers you to love others is the highest measure of renewal.

Reshaping of your spiritual personality is ultimately in the hands of the One who created your spirit. Counseling may help you to change the way you think about morality; medication may help relieve obsessive guilt—but spiritual renewal depends on the work of the Holy Spirit. It comes through an active relationship with God.

This chapter has examined six personality problems that may interfere with your relationship with God. Each one represents a longstanding misunderstanding about who you are in His eyes. Any one of them can rob you of joy and distort your spiritual identity. With a little imagination, you could probably think of 60 more such problems. Still, the answer to the 6 or 60 spirituality problems is the same—a healthy experience of God's love and power.

You can't get there on your own. You can't get enough counseling, make enough good moral choices, or even pray your way into a healthy relationship with the Father. Each of these steps are clearly helpful, but it's what God gives to us—not the thing we do—that opens the door.

In his book *Why Grace Changes Everything,* Chuck Smith, a well-known pastor, describes his preoccupation as a child with right behaviors and "getting saved again every Sunday night." He later discovered a grace that is based on a loving relationship with his Father:

> When our eyes are opened to the astonishing truth that our relationship with God does not depend on the puny pebble of our own efforts but upon the massive rock of His unchanging and loving character, life opens before us in a Technicolor explosion of awesome possibilities.[4]

A loving relationship with God the Father will sustain you through any adversity, including any periods of depressive mood. No wrongdoing from your past matters after you have changed your thinking and headed toward Him. No failure of faith causes Him to love you any less. It is your awareness of His love and your loving Him back that matter most.

Key Points

- Depression may affect the atheist, the agnostic, or the Spirit-filled Christian.
- People of faith have lower risks for depression.
- Depressive illness is not evidence of weak faith.
- Guilt can be healthy. Guilt can be unhealthy.
- A healthy spiritual personality rightly balances awareness of guilt and God's gift of forgiveness.
- Medication can restore brain function, laying the groundwork for mental and spiritual renewal.
- Spiritual health promotes emotional healing.

Part 3

SMART
Steps to Healing

Chapter 9

Recognizing Depression as an Illness

"Jesus went throughout...healing every disease
and sickness among the people."

Matthew 4:23

S omehow it's easier for people to accept the idea that depression is
a psychological or spiritual problem, not really a physical one. The
previous three chapters have talked about the spiritual and psychological perspective. You may be tempted to forget the earlier material
about the brain. Remember, very often there is a physical component
or even a physical cause of depression. Your body may need medical
intervention.

Too many good people are stuck in dark moods because they just
don't get it—sadness and irritability can be signs of brain malfunction.
Somehow we have difficulty accepting the idea that brain cells break
down, just like other parts of the body. The mysterious and powerful brain seems less vulnerable to illness and imbalance. However, all
organs—the pancreas, heart, brain—are composed of cellular units
that operate within a narrow chemical range. If we lose enough cell
function to illness or injury, the pancreas stops making insulin, the
heart loses rhythm, or the brain becomes chemically imbalanced.

Having a laboratory test for an illness makes it easier to accept diagnosis and treatment. Evidence for diabetes can be found in a test tube. High blood pressure can be detected by rising mercury. When the numbers on the gauge are abnormally high, complaints of head- ache and dizziness are seen as legitimate. We believe this person is suffering from a real problem and needs treatment.

But depression is different. Since there are currently no laboratory tests to accurately measure mood, doctors and counselors diagnose the disorder based on symptoms reported by patients. This rather subjective way of identifying depression leads some people to conclude that it's not really an illness. Although new research is helping us see the physical manifestations of mood disorders, a chemical test isn't yet available.

There are many similarities between depression and other illnesses when it comes to treatment and recovery. Healthy choices, stress reduc- tion, and spiritual commitment may reduce the need for medication. Frank Minirth and Paul Meier emphasize in their book *Happiness Is a Choice* that spiritual commitment and smart choices lift depressive moods.[1] Yet as informed physicians, they also remind readers that depres- sion can be an illness requiring medical attention. The medical side of depression becomes clear as we recognize the similarities between the illness of dark moods and more easily understood illnesses.

Depression Through the Lens of Cancer

Cancer comes in many forms—some mild, some severe. Minor skin cancers can be clipped off the nose and cured in 20 minutes. Other cancers are potentially deadly and require immediate and ongo- ing treatment. In a similar way, some depressive episodes can be cured with simple measures, while others are potentially fatal. In its worst forms, depression makes it hard to hang on to hope in the midst of fears about dying and wishes to die. Finding reasons to live can be as hard as it is when someone is diagnosed with terminal cancer.

Depression is not a cancer, but it can be fatal. Because it's a brain- cell disorder, it leads to unrealistic views of the world, poor judgment, and impulsive action. Medical treatment usually restores brain func- tion, enabling people to feel and think more realistically. Without treatment, black moods may take over. Like cancer that is caught too late, depression can be fatal. The most serious consequence of untreated depression is suicide.

I met a young scientist who refused help for depression and later died by suicide. His mother called me to ask, "What should I do?" She really seemed to be asking, "How should I feel?" Emotional confusion can overwhelm the family of a suicide victim. It feels tragic, even evil, to witness the waste of human life and the waves of grief caused in families by suicide.

Peter Kramer, in his book *Against Depression,* writes, "There is no death from illness worse for survivors than the suicide of a loved one."[2] Families and friends do not blame themselves when a loved one dies of cancer because they recognize the destructiveness of the illness and the limits of their abilities to help. Death by suicide is more complicated. Families tend to wrongly blame themselves because of unrealistic feelings of responsibility. The family who loses a loved one to cancer needs understanding and reassurance—the family who loses one to suicide needs more of the same. Some of this awful sorrow can be prevented if more people acknowledge that depression is an illness that affects the body. Medical treatment can almost always help.

Depression from the Perspective of Diabetes

Diabetes can come as a surprise. Yesterday you didn't have it but today you do. For most people, it takes a little while to accept that they now have an illness and need to do something about it. For the diabetic, *doing something* means cutting back on sugars, losing some weight, and getting more exercise. Sometimes these changes correct the chemical imbalance of insulin and blood sugar, eliminating the need for medication. Sometimes lifestyle adjustments are just not enough. When nonmedical strategies fail, the diabetic takes a pill or injection to prevent the damage from untreated illness—kidney failure, blindness, and stroke.

Depression is also a bit like diabetes. You may not have had depression last year, but you do now. It may take a while for you to accept that irritability and absence of joy can be signs of brain illness. Still, you may not need medical help to get better. Cutting back work hours, increasing recreation, and refocusing your spiritual commitment may lift you out of a mild case of depression. Yet, as with diabetes, doing all the right things may not be enough. You may need professional help to prevent the consequences of untreated depressive illness—broken relationships, loss of your job, or suicide. With excellent counseling and medication available, refusing to accept help is foolish at best— and self-destructive at worst.

Potential Consequences of Untreated Illness	
Diabetes	• Blindness • Kidney failure • Disability and death
Depression	• Job loss • Estrangement • Disability and death

Later in this part of the book, I present the SMART Steps for healing of depression. These steps offer help for healing the body, the soul, and the spirit. In order to work, they depend on your willingness to follow each of them. I urge you to consider medical care of your body just as carefully and seriously as you consider the care of your soul and spirit. Your full restoration is the goal.

Key Points

- The brain may break down physically, just like the heart, the pancreas, or joints of the leg.
- Depression may cause social and occupational handicaps.

- Sometimes the consequences of depressive illness are fatal and result in great trauma for family and friends.

- Much like treatment for diabetes or high blood pressure, lifestyle choices may reduce or eliminate the need for medication.

- It is unwise to refuse to consider professional help for depression, just as it is unwise to refuse help for cancer or diabetes.

Chapter 10
Finding Someone to Help

*"Plans fail for lack of counsel,
but with many advisors they succeed."*

Proverbs 15:22

Heather paints pictures of people who are looking out of windows, appearing to be stuck in sad places. She knows what it's like to be stuck in dark places. Before her recovery, she had lived through years of depression. When I told her I was working on this book, she asked if she could read it and offer some feedback. For her, this chapter was the most important part of it. She wrote me a note:

> Dr. Hall, chapter 10 really struck me as a chance for you to make a huge difference. I think that most counselors and psychiatrists (sorry—maybe you) do not grasp how absolutely difficult it is to find someone to help when you are really depressed. You can't just go around telling people you're depressed or suicidal and you need help. People don't know what to do with that.

Heather made suggestions, and many of her ideas are included in the pages that follow. Initial sections focus on the nuts and bolts of making the first appointment. Later sections speak to more personal aspects of picking a psychiatrist or counselor.

> ### Selecting a Doctor or Counselor
>
> 1. Get some referral names.
> 2. Consider the costs—call your insurance company.
> 3. Call selected helpers.
> 4. Evaluate your helper.

Get Some Names

Most people get referrals from their friends, their family, and their counselors. Heather got my name from a therapist. Others get suggestions from their family-practice doctor or pastor. Try to get three or four names of potential psychiatrists or therapists.

National referral networks can also be helpful. Focus on the Family, Meier Clinics, New Life Ministries, and the American Association of Christian Counselors are good sources (see page 247 at end of book). It's usually best to start the treatment process with a psychiatrist. He or she will do a comprehensive evaluation and refer you to a therapist if needed. Otherwise, you might start with a counselor. He or she can refer you to a psychiatrist if medical evaluation is needed.

Consider the Costs

It's easy to appreciate the value of a new car or a home appliance. These are tangible items that give you something to show for your money. It may not be as easy to appreciate the value of a fine dinner or a nice vacation. There is nothing to show where the money went (unless you have photos). The expense of mental-health care may be even harder to justify. There are no items to look at or pictures to enjoy. Even so, this investment has much greater potential than the previous ones to bring good things to you and your loved ones. Why not consider an investment in your mental health? Heather said,

> Because I'd been in treatment before, I was mentally prepared for the cost! Consider the cost of your last new suit or last shopping spree, and it puts things in better perspective. It's worth it!

Now, consider the nonfinancial costs and benefits. Not treating depression may lead to lost promotions, estrangements in relationships, or worse. Most people are surprised at themselves and their progress after professional treatment. A corporate executive doubled his company's holdings in one year. A middle-school teacher became principal. A lonely single woman found a loving long-term relationship. It would be misleading to suggest that everyone who gets treatment advances in some way. Clearly, that is false. It is true, however, that treatment usually leads to better performance at work and more satisfying relationships with others.

Issues of medical insurance. Nearly all health insurance policies include some coverage for mental-health treatment. The doctor or therapist you would like to see may or may not work with your insurance company.

Call the insurance company for details. Ask for information about "mental-health benefits." Expect to wait on the telephone for several minutes. Expect an automated answering system—press 1 for this or press 2 for that. Don't lose patience. You'll eventually get answers to most of your questions.

Ask the representative if the doctors or therapists you're considering are "participating providers" with that company. Services with participating providers will cost you less money, but your choices will be limited. If your selected providers aren't on their list, ask them for the names of participating providers in your area.

Then ask the representative about "out-of-network reimbursement." Will they reimburse you for expenses if you see a doctor who doesn't take your insurance? Most insurance plans provide partial reimbursement for services outside of their group. This "out-of-network option" will give you the greatest flexibility in choosing a doctor or therapist.

Some low-cost options. If you don't have medical insurance and are operating within a tight budget, you may be able to get reduced-fee service through your county mental-health department. Most county clinics offer sliding-scale payment based on your income.

For those working for large employers, another low-fee option may be available through an employee assistance program (EAP). Some employers pay for the first few visits to a therapist. Check with your human resources department.

Making the First Appointment

1. Prepare a list of 3 to 7 potential psychiatrists or counselors.
2. Call each one, one by one.
3. Ask the receptionist about:
   a. cost for each visit
   b. insurance issues
   c. appointment availability
   d. other specific issues (for example, credentials, attention to spirituality, personality)
4. Take good notes.
5. Call one of them back and make an appointment.

Make the Contacts with Doctors or Therapists, Then Investigate Further

Make a list of the helping professionals who were recommended to you, both insurance participants and nonparticipants. Consider the financial and personal aspects of seeing each one. Rank order each person according to the qualities you desire and your comfort with the cost.

Call selected helpers one by one. Ask about costs for service, insurance issues, appointment availability, and other specific questions you have. Keep calling until you get an appointment. This can be emotionally draining. Heather said it this way: "It took me a few weeks to finally find you because I could only work up the energy and courage to make a call every few days."

Starting to look deeper at the qualities of a doctor or therapist. Medication and counseling therapies are most satisfying and effective in the context of a mutually respectful relationship. Ideally, your helping professional will recognize his position as a sacred trust, being aware of the challenges you face in being open and vulnerable. Counseling and medication choices should be done *with* the patient, not given *to* the patient.

Qualities of Helping Professionals

- Professional credentials
- Caring personality
- Spiritual values

Considering three basic traits of a counselor or doctor may help you choose someone to trust. Consider *professional credentials, ability to care,* and *spiritual beliefs.* While professional credentials are important, a caring attitude and shared spiritual perspective may be equally important. For counseling that involves moral issues, the spiritual values of your therapist are more important than university credentials.

Professional credentials. Most professional counselors are trained in graduate schools and licensed by state agencies. State-licensed counselors have a master's degree or higher. They include licensed clinical social workers (LCSWs) and licensed professional counselors (LPCs). Doctoral level (PhD) therapists have four years of postgraduate education and receive internship training. Psychiatrists attend four years of medical school and obtain a doctor of medicine (MD) degree. Then they receive four more years of training in internship and residency. Most psychiatrists focus on prescribing medication. Some also practice psychotherapy.

Licensed Health Professionals' Training and Services			
Title	*Degree*	*Postcollege Training*	*Services*
Licensed Professional Counselor (LPC)	Masters (MA)	4 years	Counseling
Licensed Clinical Social Worker (LCSW)	Masters (MSW)	4 years	Counseling
Clinical Psychologist	Doctorate (PhD)	6 years	Counseling and psychological testing
Physician—General Practitioner	Doctorate (MD)	5 to 8 years	Medication
Physician—Psychiatrist	Doctorate (MD)	8 years	Medication and counseling

When selecting a doctor for medication management, the professional credentials of the physician may be more important than attitude or spiritual perspective. Any medical doctor can dispense medication. Family doctors, gynecologists, and medical specialists all treat depression as part of their practices. However, most offer short visits that permit little time for discussion of symptoms and treatment options. A psychiatrist typically spends 50 minutes evaluating the causes and consequences of depression, and is thus better able to recommend the best medication. Psychiatrists usually offer closer follow-up and attention to remission of depressive symptoms. If black moods do not promptly resolve themselves under the care of a general practitioner, the expertise of a psychiatrist should be sought. Delay of effective treatment can lead to needless job and relationship problems.

Consider training and experience

In severe or treatment-resistant depression, you'll be served better by a non-Christian psychiatrist than a Christian family physician. The training of a psychiatrist ensures a more detailed evaluation and understanding of medication effects on the brain. The more serious the impairments, the more important credentials become. Deeper and more disruptive forms of black mood call for deeper and more specific forms of training.

In choosing a physician, good training may be more important than a good heart. A Christian auto mechanic may have a loving spirit but do a poor job fixing your car. A non-Christian mechanic may do a better job fixing your transmission than someone who goes to your church. In a similar way, a caring secular professional with extensive experience may be more helpful with your depression than a Christian counselor with less training.

The importance of a caring personality. Many churches give special training to some of their members to help with emotional care of other members. The training of these "lay counselors" is variable and unregulated, but their loving support meets a clear need within the church. Gordon Allport, former head of the American Psychological Association, highlighted the importance of loving support in the counseling process, noting,

> Love—incomparably the greatest psychotherapeutic agent— is something that professional psychiatry cannot of itself create, focus, or release.[1]

As part of a caring team, lay counselors can provide prayer, encouragement, and biblical direction. A competent lay counselor will be careful to refer someone to professionals when emotional struggle becomes more serious.

Spiritual Values—A Crucial Consideration

Many of the topics of counseling will involve moral choices. Therefore, the spiritual beliefs of your therapist will be important. Her spiritual beliefs will influence the options you consider, even if you don't see it happening. While secular training teaches counselors to avoid disclosure of their personal beliefs, this is nearly impossible. When moral choices surface, a client often picks up on the verbal and nonverbal cues of a therapist. When worries involve spiritual issues, a Christian therapist will encourage a Christian client along shared value pathways. Although a secular therapist may attempt to remain neutral, she will inevitably inject personal values in unspoken ways. Some express values more openly, suggesting you explore virtually any feelings or behaviors you wish: "If you think you might like it, try it."

For this reason, many Christians are guarded about seeking counsel from secular therapists. Sometimes this hesitancy is valid, other times it isn't. Guiding clients into psychologically healthy behaviors and teaching them to manage stress more effectively can be done without addressing spiritual beliefs. Secular therapists help many people without recognizing the reality of God. Just like a non-Christian family doctor may help you overcome bronchitis, a secular counselor may help you overcome depression. However, just as a non-Christian family doctor may suggest abortion as a way to make life less complicated, a secular counselor may do the same. Hence the hesitation.

Credibility issues. This reluctance to seek help from secular counselors makes sense when you consider some of their comments. Albert Ellis, famous psychologist and proponent of cognitive therapy, commented,

> Religiosity is in many respects equivalent to irrational thinking and emotional disturbance...The elegant therapeutic solution to emotional problems is to be quite unreligious.[2]

Sigmund Freud commented that religious beliefs are "not the end result of thinking: they are illusions."[3] With comments like these, it's not hard to understand why Christians might steer clear of professional counseling.

Psychiatrists also have a credibility problem with the general public. A survey sponsored by the American Psychiatric Association found that only 13 percent of respondents had a "very positive" view of psychiatry. The public's view of ministers, priests, and rabbis, however, was not much better. The figure below shows results of a survey asking people to whom they would go to for help with emotional problems.[4] Clergy did not rank much higher than psychiatrists.

Public Opinion: Who Would You Go To for Help?	
• Family doctor	43%
• Clergy	31%
• Psychiatrist	20%
• Psychologist	16%

More reasons to be concerned about the religious perspectives of counselors comes from surveys on the importance of religion among mental-health professionals. While 70 percent of the general public agreed with the statement "My whole life is based on my religion," only 40 percent of psychiatrists and 30 percent of clinical psychologists agreed.[5] Looking on the positive side, the survey did reveal that a large portion of professional counselors do highly value their religious beliefs. Unfortunately, you may not know if your counselor is among that 30 to 40 percent.

Even with the cautions noted above, choosing a secular therapist should not be hastily rejected. They are highly trained and may provide much-needed caring support.

In recent years, the American Psychiatric Association has made some efforts to recognize the value of religion. One recent statement advised psychiatrists to inquire about a patient's spiritual beliefs "so that they may properly attend to them in the course of treatment."[6] Psychiatrists were further advised against imposing their own religious or antireligious viewpoints upon clients. These guidelines offer some reassurance, but many Christians still feel more comfortable with a Christian psychiatrist or counselor.

Sharing beliefs. Many Christians want a therapist who shares Bible-based values and incorporates these beliefs into therapy. These clients expect fewer "gaps of understanding" from a Christian therapist. A spiritually minded therapist can use scriptural helps to mend spiritual weaknesses.

The Christian counselor is sometimes seen as a sister or brother in Christ as well as a helping professional. One very cautious client, whose trust had been violated by a previous physician, told me she would not have trusted me if she had not considered me her brother in Christ.

Being identified as a Christian therapist suggests a certain way of looking at the world, but such therapists still have wide-ranging beliefs on moral issues. The figure on the next page displays results of a poll of therapists by the American Association of Christian Counselors.[7]

Christian Counselors' Moral Beliefs and Counseling Practices	
• Homosexuality is always wrong	95%
• Abortion is always wrong	76%
• Adultery, abuse, abandonment justify divorce	70%
• Counselor prays with clients every session	30%
• Divorce should never be permitted	4%

While most Christian counselors agreed with a biblical view of homosexuality, they had different opinions on several other moral choices and the role of prayer in treatment.

Counseling methods. The healing techniques and soothing interventions used by counselors vary according to their experience, but most rely on *psychodynamic* exploration and *cognitive-therapy* methods. Psychodynamic therapists encourage expression of emotions and discussion of early life conflicts. They seek to uncover life-changing experiences and hidden motivations that can be "worked through" as a way of healing. Most of these methods are not new. Long before Sigmund Freud and Carl Jung, Daniel analyzed the dreams of King Nebuchadnezzar, Christ uncovered the motivations of the Pharisees, and Paul defined the conflict between urges to do good and to do evil.

Cognitive behavioral therapy (CBT) is more focused on present-day issues. Rather than digging for roots of depression in past experience, cognitive therapists focus on problems of the here and now. CBT has formalized a commonsense approach to dealing with worries. If you are worried about flying on planes, then examine the safety records of airlines and keep these facts in your mind. If you are afraid of speaking in public, then list the realistic dangers and dismiss the unreasonable fears. CBT offers strategies to relearn these kinds of basic beliefs.

Cognitive therapists work to identify *cognitive errors* (false beliefs) and guide clients to more rational ways of thinking. Long before Aaron

Beck outlined the principles of CBT, Paul challenged the thinking of early believers and guided them though cognitive reframing, saying,

> Whatever is true, whatever is noble, whatever is right...
> think about such things (Philippians 4:8).

About Spiritually Blended Counseling

Christian counselors have adopted many of the principles of psychodynamic and cognitive therapies, blending these techniques with a religious perspective. Although these therapies make sense, they remain unproven. Blended techniques are based on personal experience and opinion, not scientific study.

Some blended therapies lead clients into a prayerful search for early life problems that may have created emotional scars.[8] Others search for distorted beliefs, which they define as lies of Satan. Clients are encouraged to confront "lie-based thinking" with biblical truth and prayer. Most psychospiritual therapists use psychodynamic approaches to uncover old hurts and cognitive-therapy techniques to confront false beliefs. Their unique value is in their emphasis on maintaining an awareness of the Holy Spirit in counseling. Most anticipate gradual and stepwise improvement. Others expect instantaneous miracles.

As with any form of healing by faith, counselors and clients must be careful to distinguish between true healing and wishful imitations. I have talked with many spiritually minded men and women who have believed for instant miracles of healing, yet ended up confused and more depressed. This happened to one Christian woman who came to my office on referral from a pastor at her church.

Becky had attended services at a healing-ministry conference and prayed for healing of depression. She had believed for healing of black moods. Most of her depression, she thought, had been caused by her husband's occult interests. She moved into an apartment to get away from his influence. She tried to keep believing in her healing but was becoming more depressed.

When doubts about her healing arose in her mind, she talked to her pastor. He referred her to me. Within a few weeks of professional counseling and medication help, her mood was calmer and her thinking clearer. This form of healing wasn't as spiritual as she would have liked, but she recognized its good fruits. She moved back into the house with her husband, and they began attending church together and finding a friendship that had been missing for years.

Our desires for miracles must be tempered with willingness to recognize that God's plans may be different than ours. Many people end up more depressed when "believing for a miracle" doesn't bring the desired outcome. We have to be careful not to confuse the shifts in our moods with the work of the Holy Spirit, and we have to be mindful not to overinterpret events in the world as signs from God. Faith is trusting in God regardless of events, not mustering up spiritual or emotional energies to create desired events.

When selecting a counselor to help you break free of dark moods, ask if she or he refers people for medication evaluation if needed. Most periods of dark mood resolve themselves without medication. Some don't. It's important that spiritually minded counselors remain open to medical ways of healing. A few counselors have wrongly advised patients to discard medications in order to demonstrate faith and be healed. This usually leads to deeper depression, not healing. Spiritual and medical helps can work together.

Hospital treatment

The hospital can serve as a safety net to catch a depressed person before someone gets hurt. For a few, those with severe depression, this is where recovery begins. It is a place of intensive evaluation and treatment. Doctors look for physical causes of black moods. Nurses and counselors teach classes on stress management. In group therapy, people learn that they aren't alone in their illness. Some hospital programs also offer art and recreation therapies to encourage emotional expression.

The idea of entering a psychiatric unit is intimidating. However, of the hundreds of people I have admitted to the hospital, nearly all have come out a great deal stronger than the day they went in. It can be a place of retreat from problems that have become overwhelming. The food isn't great and the rooms aren't fancy, but the help you get is worth some sacrifice.

Team-Building

Submitting yourself to the care of a stranger carries with it feelings of hope, apprehension, and even foolishness. It elicits mixed emotions of anticipation and hesitation. It can be exciting to know that you're finally doing something about your problem, yet may feel embarrassing to speak to a stranger about personal matters. Don't let these feelings slow you down. Self-conscious feelings disappear as the relationship develops.

Like choosing a lawyer or accountant, choosing a therapist or doctor is based on the professional and personal qualities of the helper. You have the power to start or stop the relationship any time you choose. You're the one who weighs the costs and benefits of the services you receive. Become an aggressive medical and counseling customer. Ask your friends and family for their opinions. Talk to professionals about who they know.

Then, approach your first appointment as an interview. While the therapist is forming a clinical opinion about you, you should be developing an opinion about him or her. Don't be intimidated. It's your dollar and your life. Find the counselor you feel will help. Sometimes it's prudent to meet with more than one therapist before making a commitment to continue.

When my uncle was diagnosed with stage 4 colon cancer, his doctor offered him little hope for living much longer, so he interviewed more doctors and pulled together a new health-care team—a network of medical specialists and spiritual supports. In his book *Cancer: Faith over Fear,*[9] he describes how God empowered him to take charge of his medical treatment. He sought the best treatment and, in God's time, experienced a miracle.

Whether recovering from cancer or overcoming depression, learning about your illness and taking charge of your treatment will enable you to ask the right questions of your caregivers and find the best answers. The illness of black moods can be beaten. God can guide you to the people and tools you need for recovery. Just ask. Then seek and find someone to help you get started.

Action Items

- Ask God to lead you to the helpers He has in mind.
- Get the names of three good counselors or psychiatrists from your pastor, family doctor, or trusted friend.
- Call your insurance company about in-network providers and out-of-network benefits.
- On your first appointment, interview the counselor or psychiatrist about his or her treatment approach and attention to spirituality in counseling.
- Consider meeting with a different counselor if the first one you meet doesn't seem like a good fit.
- Resolve to try counseling for several weekly visits.
- Give the helping process a little time. It may take several visits for a counselor to get to know you and develop a plan to help you.

Chapter 11

Symptoms and Diagnosis

"Why does your face look so sad when you are not ill?
This can be nothing but sadness of heart."

NEHEMIAH 2:2

When I meet a new patient, I ask a lot of questions. "Are you crying a lot...yelling at the kids...feeling helpless...hopeless? Are you taking care of your business...your family...yourself?" In the back of my mind, I work through a checklist of symptoms while offering empathy and encouragement in the process. At the end of these questions, a diagnosis becomes clear and serves as a guide for treatment.

If you or a loved one appears to be depressed, your first steps to recovery are the same. You must recognize the symptoms. Some symptoms are obvious—others require a closer look. Start by using the chart on the next page.

If you answer yes to several of these questions, then you should probably take the next step and see a caregiving professional to help you determine whether your condition represents normal responses to hardship or something more serious. If you answered yes to the question about thoughts of suicide, tell someone about those feelings and begin the process of finding someone to help right away.

Symptoms of Depressive Illness: Brief Self-Assessment		
1. Insomnia	yes	no
2. Weight loss	yes	no
3. Low energy and motivation	yes	no
4. Lost interest in pleasure	yes	no
5. Irritability	yes	no
6. Obsessive self-criticism	yes	no
7. Hopelessness	yes	no
8. Thoughts of suicide	yes	no

Common Symptoms of Depression

Most people don't seek help for depression unless they see a clear benefit—something that, if changed, would definitely improve the quality of their lives. For men, that symptom is often irritability. A doctor I see as a patient referred himself for treatment after problems with his temper led to his third broken business partnership. A problem with anger management is one of the most common reasons people come to my office. The benefits of greater patience with co-workers and family are easy to see.

Another common symptom that gets people's attention is trouble falling or staying asleep. Nearly everyone recognizes the value of a good night of sleep. Depression steals it away. Although people may not want to talk about embarrassing mental struggles, they can usually admit to poor sleep. People who would otherwise refuse to see a psychiatrist often concede that a good night of sleep might be worth the trip.

One of my patients runs a very large business. He is too busy to come in and talk about his periods of deep sadness, and he doesn't really recognize the value of talk therapy. He takes an antidepressant to get six hours of sleep and keep his mood from sliding back to angry sadness.

Memory complaints are also quite common in depression. Sometimes the memory impairments are real. More often the problems are imagined. People in the pit of depression tend to criticize themselves too much. Poor memory function is a common target of self-criticism. We all have trouble remembering things, such as phone numbers and the names of past acquaintances. People with depression also forget things, but they get stuck on their faults. They obsess over normal shortcomings.

At this point, we can learn something from my adolescent patients. Teenagers are notorious for forgetting names, assignments, and household chores. When they forget something important, they don't sit in a stew of self-pity and criticism. They forgive themselves and move on with life. Depressed adults are different. Even when memory tests are normal, people in black moods feel they're forgetting too much. This *pseudodementia,* or false dementia, is common in depression.

True memory problems, when they occur, usually stem from too much anxiety. High levels of worry almost always come with depression. Worries cloud the mind with too many things to think about. The overanxious person cannot settle down and focus on a single thing. Treatment of the underlying anxiety with counseling or medication usually returns memory function to normal.

Loss of joy. It's not always necessary to run through a checklist of symptoms to recognize depression. Asking about someone's ability to enjoy life and have a good time is also a good measure of mood. If he or she struggles to say what is fun, this may be a sign of depression. Does she like to work in the garden, spend an evening with a book, or talk with her friends on the phone? Does he like to go to the gym, tinker with tools, or strive for success at the office?

One of my patients reads math books for fun. Another finds happiness in tackle football. Both stopped doing their fun things in the midst of black moods and returned to their fun after treatment of depression.

If you are concerned that someone might be depressed, ask what he or she does to have fun. Then ask if those fun things have been happening lately. Loss of pleasure, or *anhedonia,* is a classic symptom of depression. Whether someone finds greatest joy in food, sex, or spirituality, the disappearance of these pleasure-seeking activities may signal depression.

Performance problems at work. Another way to recognize depressive moods is to look for impairments in a person's ability to work. Housewives stop their housework and builders stop their building. Projects get done poorly or don't get done at all. When people lose their abilities to work and do a good job, they've waited too long to get help.

Clinical depression is sadness to the point of disability. Somewhere between normal sadness and clinical depression, impairments creep into a person's life…one tearful day and sleepless night at a time. Job performance deteriorates. Employees get frustrated with petty differences, and bosses lose patience. Don't wait until you get fired from your job or lose an important relationship. Professional treatment of black moods can restore your abilities to love and to work.

Thoughts of suicide. Suicide is the eighth-leading cause of death in the United States. About 75 people kill themselves every day.[1] It's a severe problem that emphasizes the importance of getting help for depression.

Sliding into depression and thoughts of suicide is like falling into a pit. The hole in the ground is so cramped that you can't lift your arms to climb out. It's so dark that you see no ray of hope. The longer you stay in the pit of black moods, the more hopeless life seems. Depressed ways of thinking tell you that the world would be better off without you.

How can people whose lives seem to be full of good things consider suicide? It doesn't make sense to the average person. Somehow, though, it makes sense to the person in the pit. Absurd ideas appear reasonable. Thoughts of dying lose their significance.

A depressed bank teller described the thoughts she'd been entertaining earlier that day: "Do I want to put peanut butter on my toast or do I want to kill myself?" In her hopeless state of mind, thoughts of death didn't trigger normal responses of fear and avoidance. After her recovery, she looked back on that time with shock and amazement. "How could someone who loved life so much get stuck in that place?" she wondered out loud.

Suicidal depression is an oppressive condition. It's a time when Satan's destructive power comes face-to-face with people. Evil, sin, suffering, and destructive thoughts begin to feel unbearable. Ridiculous ways of thinking appear to make sense.

Like the altered state of a man who's had too much to drink, the chemical changes of severe depression make it hard to make good choices. If a man drinks a fifth of liquor, his ability to think straight disappears. Chemical imbalances prevent good thinking. The chemical changes of depression can be like this. As if drunk on despair, the man oppressed by black moods may step out of his rational mind.

Some people think about suicide for years before acting on their thoughts. Others talk about killing themselves in manipulative ways to gain sympathy. Still, the danger is real.

Most of the victims of suicide kill themselves in the midst of confused desperation, believing that loved ones would be better off without them. Their logic is wrong. Those left behind are not better off. Survivors always carry gnawing burdens that they should have done more.

A pilot's wife I treated for unexplained episodes of panic traced the origin of her problem back to the suicide of her cousin. Most of the time she could forget about it. But when present-day events triggered memories of the past, she would recall blood-spattered walls and become paralyzed with fear. Her cousin's selfish moment left scars in the minds of his family for years.

In the midst of deep sadness, people may not see thoughts of suicide as selfish. It is. Suicide transfers the pain of black moods onto other people. Friends and loved ones carry the pain for the rest of their lives.

Suicide takes control of suffering out of God's hands. It sabotages His plan to bring good results out of bad circumstances. Murder, including suicide, is evil. Most Christians use this understanding as an anchor to stabilize good thinking.

When I talk with people who are thinking about suicide, I try to help them reopen their eyes to the bigger picture—the world outside of their immediate suffering. Depression can be blinding. With new light on the impact of their suicide, most people open their eyes to the truth that their lives really do matter.

Suffering through valleys of depression can be seen as a man's gift to his loved ones, a good thing for the lives of others. His son will grow up knowing a father who suffers with dark moods—not weighed down by haunting memories of his death. His daughter may develop empathy for those who are suffering—not struggle with recollections of suicide. When the period of black moods has passed, the truth of these words becomes strikingly clear.

Psychotic symptoms. In periods of severe black mood, some people lose track of reality. Imagined voices and visions appear real. False beliefs about conspiracies or extraordinary powers begin to guide their behavior. Somehow the brain-cell mechanisms responsible for the orderliness of thought become short-circuited, adding false perceptions and false ideas to depressive moods. Losing the ability to distinguish voices of the imagination from voices of reality leads to enormous frustration. In order to make sense of their bizarre experiences, people make false assumptions about the world. Some become falsely convinced that people are out to get them (paranoid delusions). Others believe they have miraculous supernatural perceptions (hallucinations).

Television cartoons make the idea of imaginary voices appear humorous. They portray a character with an angel speaking in one ear and a devil speaking in the other. When we see this in a cartoon, it brings smiles to our faces. However, when people truly believe it's the voice of Satan in their ears, it's not funny at all.

For a young construction worker, depression led to a psychosis that confused his spiritual beliefs. Satan commanded Lenny to kill himself—he heard the voice as clear as any other. Then the voice of an angel told him to ignore the evil spirits and live. "All hell broke loose in my head," he said in anguish.

First, his parents took him to their pastor for prayer. They anointed his head and prayed for healing. When the voices did not end, they brought him to my office for medical help. Sometimes God heals with medication, and within two weeks, the voices vanished and depression disappeared. A delightful young man returned to my office for follow-up care.

In my care for the spiritually devout as well as the spiritually unaware, I have found that audible voices and full-field visions are symptoms of mental illness that respond quite well to medication. The fruits of these disordered "revelations" are confusion and turmoil—not encouragement or peace. The fruit of the Spirit includes peace and a sound mind—not false information or unreasonable fear. In the words of the apostle Paul,

> God has not given us a spirit of fear, but of power and of
> love and of a sound mind (2 Timothy 1:7 NKJV).

He is the architect of brain-cell design. Thank Him for His gift of medication that relieves dark moods and restores clear thinking.

Types of Depression

Psychiatrists sort depressions into two basic categories: those related to disturbing life events and those that are rooted in brain-cell problems. Although most depressive periods represent a combination of both, for purposes of discussion, diagnoses can be divided into *reactive* (event-related) or *biological* (brain-based) types.

Reactive depressions are caused by stressful events. They produce short-term changes in stress hormones and brain-cell chemistry. They don't produce long-term changes in the way the brain works. These reactive depressions resolve themselves with rest, reassurance, and the passing of time.

Biological depressions, which are rooted in brain-cell problems, result in further brain-cell injury. They may be triggered by stress, but they tend to last longer and often require medication for recovery. Each episode of brain-based depression changes the structure of brain cells and increases the risk for further depressions down the road.

Types of Depression

Event-related:
1. Normal grief
2. Adjustment disorder

Biologically-based:
1. Premenstrual dysphoric disorder
2. Major depression
3. Bipolar depression

Reactive depression. Grief is a normal reaction to a major loss. It's not a brain problem, nor is it a psychiatric disorder. The brain is doing what it was designed to do: allow a person to feel healthy sadness for a season. The initial shock and disbelief of grief may last from hours to days. Recurrent feelings of deep sadness mostly disappear within six to twelve months. Still, periods of sad reflection will usually return.

When a friend of mine lost her husband, she cried a lot and seemed distracted most of the time. She did fine at the funeral and kept up with her friendships and household duties. One lonely night, she heard the voice of her husband speaking to her from the kitchen. Hearing or seeing deceased loved ones can be a normal part of grief. Her sadness lifted several weeks later.

When the sadness that comes with loss crosses the line to become destructive depression, it becomes a psychiatric disorder. When people can't eat or get out of bed, when they begin to consider suicide, it becomes a medical problem. If the depression is the result of a specific event and lasts a short time, it may be diagnosed as an *adjustment disorder*. (See "Diagnostic Checklists" for full list of diagnostic criteria.)

The diagnosis of adjustment disorder, as you might guess from its name, describes the person who has become overwhelmed in their adjustment to stress. The word *disorder* is used because the strain of adjustment is far more than one would expect. Sadness after divorce or loss of job is normal and expected. Sadness to the point of suicidal thoughts or disability is not.

During my service as a psychiatrist in the army, I met many recruits who had difficulty adjusting to life in the military. One private was admitted to the hospital after a breakup with his girlfriend. He had unwound the spiral binding from a notebook and used the metal wire to carve the words "I love Betty Lou" into his forearm. Clearly, his reaction crossed the line that separates normal grief from a psychiatric disorder. His black moods disappeared with a few days of counseling and rest.

Biological depression. Normal sadness becomes biological depression when long-term chemical imbalances develop in the brain. Genetic predisposition makes some people more vulnerable to black moods. Emotional strain triggers chemical changes that break down brain-cell connections. Mind–brain imbalances can transform capable individuals into emotional invalids.

It's easy to see the biological side of depression when you watch how people with this brain-cell vulnerability respond to hardship. For most people, simple stress leads to minor annoyance. The same level of stress, however, triggers clinical depression in people with this brain-cell sensitivity. Chemicals responsible for managing emotion go out of balance as stress leads to changes in brain cells and tears in the eyes.

This difference in brain-cell response is like the difference in people's tendencies to bruise after injury. When one ballplayer is hit in the eye with a baseball, he experiences brief pain and no bruising. When another player is hit, he has severe pain and an ugly black eye. One ballplayer's biology is barely affected. The other player's condition is deeply changed. Biological reactions depend on a person's inherent genetic abilities to respond to stress. Some people bruise more easily. Some people get depressed more easily.

Many medical-insurance companies recognize the difference between brain-based and event-related depression. They recognize that people with biological depressions, such as major depressive disorder and bipolar disorder, need more professional help. Although they may limit the treatment of reactive depressions to perhaps 20 visits per year, this cap doesn't usually apply to brain-based depressions.

Brain-based depression in women. Most men know, but don't really understand, how a woman's mood can change back and forth in just a few days. We recognize that women in our families sometimes get moody for no apparent reason. But it's rising and falling levels of hormones that tip the balance of brain chemistry once a month and make them more sensitive to stress.

It is quite normal for moods to go down in the week before menstruation. Premenstrual syndrome (PMS) is not a psychiatric disorder—it's a common type of mood fluctuation. About 80 percent of women have at least one symptom of PMS during the week before menses. Symptoms may include sadness, irritability, and hunger for carbohydrates. Symptoms usually resolve themselves in five to ten days.

When these changes in mood get intense and interfere with daily activities, they are considered diagnostic symptoms of premenstrual dysphoric disorder (PMDD). PMDD is a magnified form of PMS affecting about 5 percent of women of childbearing age.

When a friend referred his wife to me for treatment of premenstrual mood swings, they were both ready for some help. He had done some online research on PMDD and discussed the diagnosis with his wife. She was ready for some kind of intervention because she saw how the mood swings were driving her loved ones away. She began treatment with a serotonin-enhancing antidepressant, which restored balance to her emotions and harmony in her home.

In the past, gynecologists treated this disorder with hormone replacements but found the results disappointing. Now most of them use serotonin-based antidepressants that work quite well.

Another period of vulnerability to biologically based depression is during the months after childbirth. Wide fluctuations of hormones may cause women to be cranky, irritable, and tearful. This is normal. About 70 percent of women experience *postpartum blues* within two weeks of delivery. Symptoms usually resolve themselves without mental-health treatment.

Postpartum depression is something different—a serious psychiatric diagnosis affecting about 10 percent of women within a few weeks of delivery. In its most severe form, postpartum depression can lead to psychotic thinking. Hallucinations and delusions can lead to dangerous behaviors resulting in the death of mother and infant. *Postpartum psychosis* affects less than 1 percent of new moms. *It should be considered a psychiatric emergency.* A new mom with postpartum depression should be referred for professional help. It's a serious problem that is relatively easy to treat and control.

A tearful young mother rolled her stroller and baby into my office. A little overweight from the pregnancy and a lot overwrought by child care, she remained on the verge of tears most of the time. She sat down on the chair next to my desk and immediately began looking for a box of tissues. It didn't make sense to her. I assured her that her symptoms did make sense and suggested a plan of medication and counseling. She returned two weeks later with a beaming smile on her face and praised me as some kind of miracle worker. (I must confess I enjoyed this praise, since we were walking down the hallway within earshot of my colleagues.)

Major depressive disorder. This is the big one—the diagnosis most people are talking about when they speak of clinical depression. Some diagnostic symptoms were listed in the brief self-assessment on page 118. (See "Diagnostic Checklists" for a full list of criteria.)

In severe cases of major depressive disorder, people look like they're having a "nervous breakdown." A perky cosmetic clerk can be turned into a sorrowful puddle of tears. A confident, burly carpenter can be transformed into a helpless recluse. Thinking and emotional abilities collapse.

When conditions are mild to moderate, people may not recognize the signs of illness for several years. When they finally break free, they often remark about their failure to do something sooner. Some had been depressed so long that they didn't even remember joy. Sadness for them had become normal.

Many patients describe an awkward excitement at recovery. Guarding their enthusiasm, they quietly worry that good feelings won't last. They smile with relief as I tell them that the return of joy most often continues. A more natural mix of good days and bad days replaces a chronically unhappy outlook.

Bipolar disorder. This is the most complicated type of depression. Diagnosis of bipolar disorder includes two characteristics. First is the presence of *manic cycles*—moods and energy get too high. Second is the presence of *major depressive disorder cycles.* Moods alternate between periods of deep sadness (depressive pole) and periods of great energy (manic pole). Hence the name *bipolar.*

In mania, people often feel bigger than life. They appear more vital and enthusiastic than the average person. They talk too fast, think too fast, and can't turn off their minds to go to sleep. This usually leads to poor judgment and impulsive behaviors they live to regret.

Distinguishing bipolar depression from *unipolar* depression (that is, major depressive disorder) is very important before selecting a treatment. Prescribing antidepressants to someone with bipolar depression can actually make that person worse because people with bipolar depression are highly sensitive to them.

While antidepressants elevate the mood of the person with regular depression, in the person who is depressed because of bipolar disorder, they may cause an overshoot of normal and bring on manic excitement. Antidepressants lift energy too far. People with bipolar depression need

medication to stabilize their mood and prevent manic overshoot—
before they start to use an antidepressant.

A teacher I know lost her job because her general practitioner treated
her unrecognized bipolar depression with antidepressant alone. Her
mood shot up into mania. She had too much excitement and impul-
sivity to keep order in the classroom. She made bad choices with her
students and got into fights with the principal. I met her after she
had been discharged from a psychiatric hospital. We started mood-
stabilizer medication to settle her mind—but too late to repair her
reputation or save her job.

Diagnosis of depression can be complicated. Many states of sadness are normal; some are even healthy. Others are quite destructive.
It takes time and experience to sort out the various types, especially
in bipolar depression. For diagnosis of depression, the office of a psychiatrist or clinical psychologist is the best place to start.

Diagnostic Puzzles

Stan is an intern who's training in our office. He's learning to diagnose and treat depression by thinking about diagnosis as constructing
a puzzle. His puzzle approach provides a helpful illustration about how
diagnoses are made.

When he meets a new patient, all the pieces of the puzzle are face-
down. As the interview proceeds, individual pieces are turned over.
Personal experiences add color and clues to that person's emotional
history and counseling needs. By the end of a diagnostic interview,
he can usually assemble enough pieces to get a good picture of that
person's emotional life.

As with a jigsaw puzzle, not every piece is needed to get the big
picture. Some pieces, however, are more critical than others. Suicide
thoughts, substance abuse, and destructive relationships are indispensable. If they're present, they must be found. They serve as guides to
developing a plan for recovery.

The SMART Steps model that is described in the next chapter will outline a plan for renewal. The pictures that are formed by the jigsaw puzzles of today can be exchanged for brighter pictures of tomorrow.

Action Items

- Examine the checklists in this book to see if you should consider diagnosis and treatment of depression.
- Inability to work or maintain loving relationships are just as important as checklist symptoms.
- Hormone fluctuations create greater risks for depression in women, especially in postpartum periods.
- Take thoughts about suicide seriously. If you are thinking about this permanently wrong solution to a temporary and treatable problem, get some help now.
- If you can recall periods of very high energy lasting more than one week despite very little sleep, consider the diagnosis of bipolar depression. You may need a psychiatrist to help you develop a plan for stabilizing and lifting your mood.

Chapter 12

The SMART-Step Model

"A prudent man gives thoughts to his steps."

PROVERBS 14:15

I wish they knew that people really do get better," she said. After 15 years of black moods, a kindhearted country-store clerk broke free of depression. Glenda again delighted in going to tractor pulls with her husband, found pleasure in chatting with neighbors at the store, and realized more than ever that God had been with her all the time. Enthusiasm compelled her to share the good news: "People really do get better." But it helps to have a good plan.

SMART Steps

This part introduces the SMART plan for renewal, offering a fly-over view of changes to come. The next five chapters will add details to the picture, beginning with step S and ending with step T. As with building a pyramid, each new phase of development is dependent on the construction of a firm foundation in previous stages.

This model blends medical, mental, and spiritual ingredients into a holistic process of recovery. It illustrates how your spiritual health is the most vital when it's built on strong physical and mental foundations.

Recovery from depression is most complete when approached from an integrated mind–body–spirit perspective.

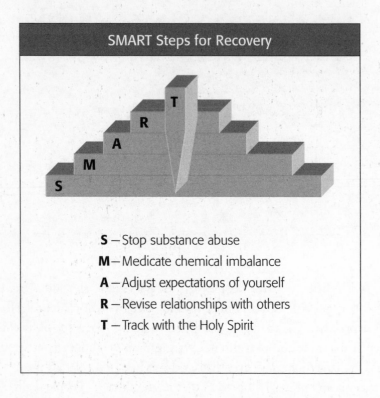

SMART Steps for Recovery

S – Stop substance abuse
M – Medicate chemical imbalance
A – Adjust expectations of yourself
R – Revise relationships with others
T – Track with the Holy Spirit

Stop Substance Abuse

Many people begin at step S—*stop substance abuse*. Others try medication, psychotherapy, or spiritual pursuit without letting go of addiction—failing to recognize that therapeutic helps do not work in a brain that is clouded by substance abuse.

For those dependent on alcohol or drugs, the first step is to break the depression–addiction connection. Substance abuse damages brain cells and can lead to depression. Ironically, many people attempt to self-medicate depression with alcohol, adding to biological injuries. They wrongly assume that alcohol will help them sleep at night and cope with hard days. The opposite effect occurs because alcohol disrupts sleep patterns and leads to denial of the importance of daily problems.

Glenda, the country-store clerk, had a problem with prescription-medication abuse. For her, renewal began when she resolved to stop. She admitted the problem to herself, confessed her addiction to me, and joined a 12-step recovery group. Without the impairments of drug abuse, she found that antidepressants and counseling began working, and that people really can get better.

Medicate the Chemical Imbalance

The second SMART step in breaking free of depression is to *medicate the chemical imbalance* (if present). Just as medical treatment of high blood pressure is sometimes necessary, treatment of depression may require medical adjustment. And just as lifestyle changes may resolve hypertension, lifestyle responses to depression may be enough to correct the chemical imbalance. When in doubt, talk to a professional about the pros and cons of using medication.

When mood messengers misfire, as we saw earlier, mental processing slows down. This makes it difficult to think of solutions and to participate in counseling. Medication can help heal your brain. You'll improve your ability to think of answers to relationship problems and challenges at work.

Talking to a counselor and seeking help from her church were not enough for Glenda. She needed a medical correction to her chemical imbalance to regain sharpness in thinking and stability of mood. With her brain cells recharged, she's managing customers at work with new confidence and is more involved in the lives of her children.

Adjust Expectations of Yourself

For people who don't have a substance-abuse problem or signs of chemical imbalance, recovery from depression starts here at step three—*adjusting expectations*. This step starts with exploring your worries, then looking beneath the surface for unreasonable expectations. Some people expect too much of themselves, others too little. One of the most important mental steps in recovery is developing a more realistic sense of your responsibilities through self-examination or counseling.

In therapy, Glenda relaxed her exaggerated expectations about how safe or happy she could make herself or anyone else. She learned to adjust childhood vows and childhood resignations, developing a more balanced view of herself and her place in the world. She no longer tries so hard to be the opposite of her mother or to prove that she's really a good person. Adjusting expectations has reduced her frustration, helped her relax, and reduced the amount of stress hormones bombarding her brain.

Revise Relationships with Others

The fourth step begins a process of *revising relationships,* which includes expressing your feelings, granting forgiveness, and building new boundaries. Confronting dysfunctional relationships in these ways may increase your stress in the short term but reduce your conflicts in the long run.

Expressing bad feelings is a form of catharsis. Just like vomiting can be cathartic after eating spoiled meat, expressing bad feelings through words can produce healthy release. But also like vomiting in the wrong place may create an aggravating mess, expression of bad feelings in the wrong way can make matters worse.

After speaking your mind, consider a process of forgiveness. This book outlines a seven-step process starting with emotional expression and ending with setting up boundaries. In the middle are steps of discovering what has hurt you and how to forgive 70 x 7 times. At the end, building new boundaries brings closure to the process of revising relationships, with the goal of establishing mutual respect.

Spiritual Renewal

The ultimate goal of the entire SMART renewal plan is to line out a pathway from clinical depression to spiritual vitality. In one sense, a healthy relationship with God is the climax of spiritual vitality.

In another sense, a relationship with Him should infuse each other step.

From the first perspective, *tracking with the Holy Spirit*—the "T"—is the pinnacle of recovery. An intimate relationship with God, made possible through His Spirit, makes concerns about brain cells and self-esteem appear like meaningless distractions.

From the second point of view, recovery involves a complicated set of choices that should be directed by prayerful searching. God's Spirit can guide you to the right counselor, physician, and spiritual influences that will enable you to fulfill the plan He has for your life. Spiritual vitality adds strength and direction to the other four steps.

Glenda's path seemed gloomy and obscure during early months of her quest. She continued to pray, even when her words seemed to bounce off the walls or drift into a void of nothingness. Her breakthrough came in God's time and way. Now she celebrates recovery and shares in the joyful faith of the children she teaches in Sunday school.

Guideposts, Not Requirements

The SMART Steps are guideposts, not rigid requirements. While this model is a stepwise plan, don't wait for perfection at one stage before moving to the next. Begin working on the first step while you set your eyes on the next. All steps should be considered and reconsidered many times along the way.

It's smart to begin with step S. If you have a problem with substance abuse, then your progress through steps M-A-R-T will be difficult or impossible. While relationship conflicts often lead people into counseling, clients are sometimes disappointed when their counselor's focus changes from problems with the girlfriend to problems with drinking. Relationship troubles are rarely resolved when one partner continues to abuse alcohol or drugs.

There are also good reasons to start with Step M if necessary. You'll need your best thinking to manage the problem of depression. Some people wait too long, getting stuck on counseling issues for years without seeing the need for medication. Even therapists sometimes delay too long. When six months of marital counseling ends in divorce, it's too late to consider the benefits of medical treatment for irritability.

The principles discussed in steps A and R are guideposts for stress management and personal growth, as well as re-emergence from depression. They're important whether you suffer from dark moods or not.

The final step is T. It is both the beginning and the end of black-mood breakthrough for the believer.

Whether you think of treatment in this stepwise process or not, your therapist will probably address these elements in her or his way. Many therapists refuse to begin counseling if a client refuses to stop drinking. Most are aware of the right time and place for medication. Christian counselors and ministers take the process further, encouraging spiritual renewal in the process.

As Glenda said, "People really do get better."

Action Items

- Set a goal for yourself to feel remarkably better by this time next year.
- Keep your eyes on the goal.
- Patiently and deliberately work through the SMART Steps.
- Read Isaiah 40:28-31 and believe that God is waiting to give you the strength to rise up like an eagle and soar.

Chapter 13

Stop Substance Abuse

*"Like a city whose walls are broken down is a
man who lacks self-control."*

PROVERBS 25:28

R ecovery from addiction is like tending a garden. Bad habits are
like weeds, and you're like the gardener. This chapter will help
you examine the habits that are growing in your life and suggest some
tools for digging them out.

While much of this chapter focuses on addiction to alcohol, the
principles of recovery apply to breaking other bad habits as well. Most
people struggle with something—an unhealthy habit they wish they
could stop. Some are dependent on drugs. Others rely too much on
sex, food, or money. The pathways to recovery are very much alike.

The Depression–Addiction Connection

Depression and addiction often grow together. Alcohol is the most
common addiction among those with black moods. In the U.S., the risk
of becoming dependent on alcohol is about 15 percent.[1] That means that
15 of 100 adults in the U.S. will develop problems with alcohol at some
point in their lives. For people with depression, the risk of alcohol problems
nearly doubles, becoming a cause and a consequence of black moods.

As one condition worsens, the other often follows. Alcohol injures brain cells, increasing the risk of depression. In the opposite way, the chemical imbalance that comes with depression can lead to poor judgment, impulsive action, and alcohol abuse. It happened that way for a taxi driver named Joe.

"I started drinking because I didn't like the world," he explained. "It didn't help."

"My problems got worse."

"In the end, I didn't like myself."

One vodka binge led to two and two led to ten. Joe's moods grew dark and desperate as he began planning to end his life. In the sickness and sadness of that moment, he reached out for help. He called a friend and his friend called me.

Joe humbled himself and came to my office. We talked about past choices and how to make better ones, about his mixed-up feelings and attempts to escape them through drinking. In counseling and soul-searching, he found better ways to cope. Antidepressants helped to restore his ability to think straight. He joined a group of recovering alcoholics who gave him support and helped relieve feelings of loneliness. Using all the tools he could find, Joe broke free of addiction and black moods.

Freedom did not come in one day or two weeks of counseling. It came by holding on to his resolution to make a better way, by repeating the same right choices day after day.

How Much Is Too Much?

> Who has woe? Who has sorrow? Who has strife? Who has complaints? Who has needless bruises? Who has bloodshot eyes? Those who linger over wine (Proverbs 23:29-30).

When does a little wine with dinner or a few beers with friends turn into alcohol dependence? When do good times and good drinks become addiction? The line between casual drinking and addiction can become blurry.

A checklist of problems associated with drinking is found in "Signs of Alcohol Dependence" on page 234. Looking over this list may help you recognize the impact of your habits. Maybe you need to make your own list. Think about how your habit is affecting others and yourself as you consider the following questions:

1. What do you most regret about your habit?
2. When were you the most embarrassed?
3. When were you most sick of yourself?
4. Who have you hurt?
5. Who could get hurt?
6. How?
7. Does the habit affect your work?
8. What is it doing to your body and spirit?
9. What are the dangers of continuing?

Spend some thinking about your list of consequences. Return to your list tomorrow, keeping the bad outcomes fresh in your mind. It will help you find motivation for healthier choices.

Denial

Bad habits continue because people find excuses to do the bad thing one more time. Most of the excuses are simply tactics to delay hard choices. Some of the excuses are sadly amusing.

A bushy-haired mechanic told me that he planned to quit drinking, and then described his plan to get drunk one more time to celebrate his sobriety. Addiction makes smart people say silly things. He did not quit that day or the next.

A pretty young woman came to my office for help stopping cocaine. I asked about how she planned to quit. The first step, she explained, was to move in with her boyfriend. He was a drug-dealer.

"He understands my problem," she said.

"He knows about drugs."

"He is the best one to help me stop."

Addictions make bright people say stupid things. This woman refused to truly recognize her problem or the dangers of being around cocaine. She moved in with her boyfriend and did not return for her next appointment. Slowly and deceptively, addiction and denial separated Linda from her loved ones and her own good sense.

The Challenge

Breaking bad habits can be hard. Most people fail. Research shows that 40 to 70 percent of people who try to break an addiction will relapse within a year.[2] This includes both people who try to do it on their own and those who seek help. Even 30-day rehabilitation programs do little to improve these sobering statistics. Most people who complete rehab programs relapse within 90 days.[3]

Before getting pessimistic, focus on the fact that 30 to 60 percent break free. They become part of a grateful minority. For you to do the same, you will probably need help.

Willpower helps. Alone, it will most likely fail.

Alcoholics Anonymous (AA) can help. Alone, it will probably fail.

Spiritual commitment may help. Addiction can be broken in a moment by faith but more often God works with people over time.

When depression and addiction come together, antidepressants can help. However, using medication without counseling or group support usually fails.

Breaking bad habits is hard. Relapse is easy. The challenge is to keep making the right choices day after day, using all of the spiritual, social, and professional tools that God provides.

Recovery Tools

Keeping a nice garden is a process. It requires pulling up the weeds and nurturing the flowers. In a similar way, recovery from addiction is a process of plucking out bad habits and nurturing healthy habits. Both gardening and recovery are made easier by using the right tools.

God is the source of all good things, including the tools that you need for recovery. He knows your heart and your personal struggle and has a plan for renewing your mind. Prayer can reveal His plan and give you the power to realize His goals.

Counselors and friends can also be tools of recovery. Breaking an addiction, like weeding a garden, can be lonely at times. The job is made easier when someone is working beside you.

Medications can be tools. Antidepressants are helpful when depression and addiction are growing in the garden together. Changing a bad habit takes energy—something sorely missing in depressive illness. Antidepressants help restore vitality to the person working through the process of recovery.

Using spiritual tools.

> Each one is tempted when, by his own evil desire, he is dragged away and enticed. Then, after desire has conceived, it gives birth to sin; and sin, when it is full-grown, gives birth to death (James 1:14-15).

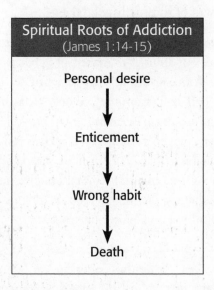

Look in the mirror—straight into your eyes. Examine your heart. The root of addiction is somewhere in there.

Temptation comes to each of us. It is the choice that we make at the point of enticement that matters. If we dismiss the enticement and go another way, desires will diminish—habits of making good choices will take shape. If we allow the enticements to linger, desires will carry us into destructive behaviors.

Healing from addiction starts in the same place—the place where enticements become desires. This is a good place to begin.

First, ask God to work on your heart. Acknowledge and change your mind about wrong desires, and be willing to pray something like this:

"God, clean up my heart."

"Remove my desire for _____ and renew a right spirit in me."

Now, change your thinking. Be careful with your imagination. Step way from temptation and move your mind to some other thought. There are plenty of healthy things to think about. Think on them. Rehearse healthy thoughts. Repeating spiritually good thoughts will nurture the growth of spiritually good habits.

Digging up weeds with prayer. God uses prayer to uproot wrong thinking and empower our abilities to make right choices. Begin with the "Lord's Prayer." Notice how Christ asked for help: "Lead us not into temptation, but deliver us from the evil one" (Matthew 6:13). Christians, like Christ, need help overcoming temptation.

Now, consider a prayer of sacrifice. As much as you are able, give the pleasure of your habit to God. For one hour, one day, or longer, choose to step away. In your moment of temptation, give up the pleasure of indulging that habit as a sacrifice to God. Settle this commitment in your mind by thinking on a prayer like this:

God
I bring a sacrifice.
I give up _____, for this hour/day.
I give this habit to You.
Forgive me, and clean up my heart.

Pray this prayer each hour of the day at the start of recovery. Speak these words each day as you recover and new ways of thinking begin filling your mind.

As you begin to make progress, consider a prayer of gratitude, recognizing that the One who began His good work in you is committed to complete it. Thank Him:

> Thank You for freedom from _____
> and restoring my power to make right choices.
> Thank You for wisdom
> and the example of Christ.
> Thank You for Your Holy Spirit
> who keeps my recovery going one day at a time.

Planting Good Seeds

Along with good tools, you will need some good seed for your garden. As you dig out the weeds of bad habits, look for some healthy replacements. Plant some seeds that will sprout into better behaviors. Inspirational books can be sources for these seeds; so can spiritual songs and the encouraging words of a friend.

The best source for seeds is the Expert Gardener. Read His gardening book. The Bible is full of good idea-seeds. Consider how Paul encouraged the Romans to turn away from wrong, and then apply his words to your own struggle. Read the first two verses of Romans chapter 6, then read them again as you substitute the name of your bad habit for the word "sinning."

> What shall we say, then? Shall we go on _____ so that
> grace may increase? By no means! We died to _____ ;
> how can we live in it any longer? (Romans 6:1-2).

Then read the rest of this chapter. The words clearly reveal that we have access to God's power that raised Christ from the dead—spiritual power that restores newness of life.

For new ideas to grow into new behaviors they must be acted out.

> ### Spiritual Gardening Tips
>
> 1. Weed: dig out bad habits
> 2. Seed: plant good idea-seeds
> 3. Feed: nurture new behaviors

Ideas need encouragement to grow into habits. If spiritual commitments begin to sprout, then water them with prayer. If healthy relationships begin to sprout, then feed them by being with other Christians. If a passion for exercise begins to grow, then hop on a treadmill or get to a gym.

As new behaviors mature, they will yield seeds of their own. Spiritual habits will yield spiritual seeds. Emotional growth will yield seeds of self-esteem and deepening friendships. As right behaviors continue to bear seeds, good idea-seeds will begin falling into the lives of people around you. Your life will become a source for good seeds that take root in the hearts of others.

A perspective on Satan's role. Satan scatters seeds of destruction. He scatters idea-seeds that grow into damaging behaviors. He is the angel of the abyss, whose name is destroyer (see Revelation 9:11). He is a liar. He secretly seduces and destroys.

> Our struggle is not against flesh and blood, but against...
> the powers of this dark world and against the spiritual forces
> of evil in the heavenly realms (Ephesians 6:12).

A really nice young man was seduced and destroyed by alcohol. Drinking had relieved his worries for a while, but one night of alcohol-escape became two...Within a few months, he was drinking a fifth of liquor each day. His family tried to help. They referred him to me. He reluctantly entered a rehabilitation program and then dropped out. One year later, his sister called to tell me that Sam had died of alcohol poisoning.

Was it Satan's seduction that ruined his life? Was it the self-deifying nature that's present in each of us? I don't know. I do know that Sam was deceived into exchanging healthy pleasures for destructive habits. He believed the lie that "doing it one more time will be okay."

There is a better way. The good and everlasting news is that God is greater. He is our protector and deliverer. By keeping our eyes on Him and looking for His way, we can find freedom from bad habits.

A different young man found help in his struggle. His attempts to break a destructive habit were failing until he reached out to God. Jerry came to my office for help with depression. Initially, he refused to talk about his use of cocaine. He wanted to talk about his frustrating moods and marital problems. I explained the depression–addiction connection and that the first step in overcoming black moods would be stopping his heavy use of cocaine (Step S of SMART renewal). We talked about his joining Narcotics Anonymous (NA). He dismissed the idea:

"Too many messed up people in those groups, and too much talk about God."

"Those meetings make me feel like doing drugs," he complained.

Jerry wasn't ready for help. He had been enticed and seduced by short-term pleasures, so he didn't return for his next week's appointment.

One month later Jerry stumbled into my office, clothes muddy and eyes full of despair. This time he knew he would lose his family if he didn't stop his addiction. With tears streaming down his face, he cried, "If I don't get some help, I'm screwed."

We talked about the mess and ways to get clean. We talked about treatment options, NA and spirituality. He paused.

"Why would God want me now? Tomorrow I may go out and do it again!"

We talked about deep change of mind, forgiveness, and mercy. This time Jerry was ready. He opened his heart, and God came in. He discovered recovery through spiritual tools and counseling. Enticements pop up, but he continues to pray and wait for God's answers, leaning on his powerful Ally.

Daily bread. Gardening is hard work. Building new habits takes energy. God provides power to make good choices one day at a time.

Jesus prayed, "Give us this day our daily bread."

He did not ask for bread for next week or strength for tomorrow. He teaches us to ask for His nourishment one day at a time. God provides "spiritual bread" one day at a time. Some days He gives wheat bread, sometimes it's white. One day His bread is packaged in the word of a friend. Another day it comes through a verse of the Bible. Some days His power comes through an unexpected event. Other times daily bread comes in a capsule of medication. God has many types of daily bread to keep your recovery going. He knows what we need for today.

Psychological Tools

Sometimes recovery comes with the help of counseling and self-examination—developing new habits through mental exercise. In many ways, recovery is a process of relearning basic common sense.

In one of my psychology classes, our assignment was to teach a white mouse a new habit. I taught my little mouse to climb a toy ladder and slide down a board. He learned to repeat this behavior because I enticed and rewarded him with food. Each step up the ladder brought a treat. Each slide down the board got him another. My classmates laughed as they watched his amusing behavior.

People also do silly things for pleasure. One "harmless" night of fun starts the process. Repeated "harmless" pleasures build destructive habits. People, like mice, slide down slippery slopes.

I learned another lesson about habits in that class. When a mouse is given a choice between cocaine and food, the mouse will choose cocaine again and again. He'll indulge the bad habit until he dies of exhaustion. Mice have a lot in common with people. "Harmless" little pleasures can become destructive daily patterns.

Think about your own enticements. What are the morsels that reinforce your own bad behavior? What reinforces your unhealthy use of alcohol, drugs, or sex? Make a list of the mental steps that lead you up the ladder, then start saying no to the little morsels that lead you up the ladder and down the slippery slope.

Rebuilding walls. Rebuilding self-control is like constructing a wall. To build a strong wall, you'll need a lot of good bricks. The wall will be built one brick at a time. While one single brick does not seem like much on its own, when it's stacked alongside others it creates a strong barrier. To rebuild self-control, you will need to put together a lot of good choices.

A new habit is built one choice at a time. While saying no to one little morsel of enticement may not seem like much, lining up good choices one after another can build an impressive barrier of self-control. Each time you say no adds a brick to the wall. Every refusal to indulge enticement adds another brick. Each moment of self-denial adds a brick. Stepping away from temptation adds a brick.

Start laying down bricks to re-establish self-control. If you drink too much, stop going to the bar. Keep a healthy distance between you and temptation. If drugs are your weakness, stop hanging around the people who use them. Keep a closed door between you and a relapse.

Refuse to linger on temptation. Add a brick. Stop looking for opportunities to indulge a bad habit. Move your imagination to something better—plug a hole in the wall. Keep saying no, and the wall will get stronger. One choice becomes two choices, and many choices become a habit. New ways of responding to temptation will become engrained in your lifestyle.

Saying yes to temptation has the opposite effect—wall-busting. It knocks a brick out of the wall. Do it again and the holes will get bigger. The wall will begin to crumble and self-control will break down. Weeds will get in and addiction takes over.

It's too late for moderation. If playful flirtation has become a destructive habit, then it's too late for "just one more time." A compulsive overeater cannot have "just one more" bite of strawberry pastry. An alcoholic cannot have "just one more" drink. One drink leads to two and two drinks to ten. There are few exceptions. Knock out one brick and the second is easier to dislodge. Knock out some more bricks and addiction creeps in. "Just one more time" is not an option when changing a bad habit.

Four building blocks. You'll need some bricks to rebuild the wall of self-control. Begin with some basic building blocks that add with strength and stability. Four basic construction materials are summarized in the acronym HALT.

- **H** is for hungry. Don't let yourself get too hungry. Have a piece of fruit or a handful of nuts. Healthy food can create a sense of satisfaction and diminish the urge to indulge a bad habit. Add a brick.
- **A** is for angry. Don't get stuck in anger. Unpleasant feelings can become a trigger for relapse. They create a sense of urgency that something must be done right now. That is usually not true. Pause. Talk to somebody. Put your feelings into words, and your emotions will settle and patience return. Express yourself with words and seek peace. Add a couple more bricks to the wall.
- **L** is for lonely. Don't spend too much time alone. It creates vulnerability to temptation. Like a burning stick of wood that's separated from others loses its flame, too much time alone may diminish your passion for recovery. Get to know other healthy people and let others get to know you. Add a few more bricks to the wall.
- **T** is for tired. Don't get run down. Take a nap. Close your eyes. Stretch out your legs for a while. Pick a good bedtime and get some good sleep. A restful night of sleep makes the challenges of tomorrow easier to manage, restoring energy and a healthy outlook. Add another brick to the wall.

Habit replacement. Getting rid of a bad habit will create empty space in your day. You'll have more time and energy for other things. So look for some healthy new ways of thinking and behaving to fill up that empty space.

Learn how to have fun again. Addicts forget how to have fun without the bad habit. Remember that it's quite possible to enjoy a football game without a beer. It can be relaxing to watch a movie without chemical enhancement. If you've forgotten how to have fun, think about children. A seven-year-old child knows how to find fun.

Think back. You knew how to find clean fun in the past. Bring back the healthy habits. Exercise. Get together with people. Read a book, or make something with your hands. Dust off those old healthy behaviors and do them again.

Both good habits and bad habits produce long-term changes in the brain. Those old ways of thinking are ingrained in your brain-cell network. If you were a golfer, you'll always have a tendency to golf, making it easier for you to seek pleasure in that way. If you are an addict, you will always be inclined to indulge that bad habit—it's hardwired into the chemistry of your brain.

Your brain has been changed. The sight of a beer or a sexually enticing picture will trigger unwanted excitement in unguarded moments. Your brain has patterns of response to specific enticements. Keep plucking out the weeds as they sprout.

In the past, you looked forward to indulging bad habits. Now it's time to anticipate healthy pleasures and fall back into good habits. Go for a walk or have lunch with a friend. As you repeat healthy pleasures, you will begin to appreciate and anticipate them more.

Social Tools

Addiction grows in the dark. Recovery begins in the light. Revealing your problem to someone else sheds light on the problem and opens your mind to new directions. Some people get help in groups. Others do better in private counseling. Look for someone you can trust, who will support your passion for renewal.

Recovery groups. Joining a support group provides a place for accountability and encouragement. Most recovery groups emphasize confidentiality—what's said in the group stays in the group. Many are based on the 12 steps of Alcoholics Anonymous (AA).[4]

AA is a network of everyday people who fell into addiction and found a way out. They find purpose for living and strength for right choices in helping other people to make the same choices. It is a fellowship of spiritual and behavioral change.

People in AA speak of a "Higher Power" that can help them stop drinking. Christians know this Higher Power as God. He gives us forgiveness through His Son and power through His Spirit. Spiritual belief and commonsense ideas are woven together in the 12 steps of AA. The "Serenity Prayer" is popular in AA because it illustrates this blending of spiritual perspective and practical choice:

> God grant me the serenity
> To accept things I cannot change,
> Courage to change the things I can,
> And wisdom to know the difference.[5]

The first three steps of recovery in AA parallel the biblical principles of salvation. Step 1 is recognizing our powerlessness to control a deeply ingrained habit on our own, which is like recognizing our inability to save ourselves from evil and wrongdoing. The second step of AA is acknowledging that a Higher Power can help break the bad habit, which is like recognizing that God has power to rescue us from evil. The third step is surrendering ourselves and the problem to that Higher Power, which is like giving our lives, the good and the bad, to God.

Spirituality is prominent in some AA groups, but it's not the main purpose of the group. The primary purpose of AA is to keep people

Spiritual Perspectives on the 12 Steps of AA	
AA Step	*Spiritual Perspective*
1—Accept powerlessness	"I can't"
2—Recognize Higher Power	"He can"
3—Surrender the problem	"I give it to Him"

sober one more day, not lead them to Christ. If you want to get closer to Jesus, then develop a habit of prayer and find a Christ-centered church. If you want support for sober thinking, then go to AA.

When I meet a new patient who wants to break addiction, I breathe a sigh of relief when he agrees to join a recovery group. Attending a group doesn't guarantee success. The risk for relapse is high no matter what he does. Even so, joining a recovery group is a sign of commitment and provides help with the weeding and feeding of behavioral change.

When I met Brittany, she had a problem with alcohol but denied signs of addiction when I asked her. Several months later, her daughter came into their living room and found her drunk on the couch, surrounded by piles of beer cans. A month after that, she got into a brawl with her equally intoxicated cousin. Broken and ashamed, she told me of her "hidden" addiction. We talked about treatments.

I was immediately relieved when she agreed to go to AA. She found help with those people. She smiled again. She stayed sober. She learned to manage bad feelings and smiled some more. She made some new friends. They went to lunch and stayed sober together. They went to the store and attended more meetings. She rediscovered how to enjoy life in a sober state of mind.

Counseling. While support groups like AA work very well for many people, some need individual counseling. Combining group support with one-on-one counseling is often most helpful.

The early months of recovery can be marked by large swings of emotion. Initial feelings of excitement may be washed away by cravings and regrets. Angry and frustrated feelings, once blocked by substance abuse, are unleashed. Counseling can help manage this new awareness of emotion.

Sometimes it hurts to see things as they are. It seems easier to pretend that some bad thing did not happen, ignoring the hurt. Substance abuse is one way to cover up feelings—to emotionally pretend that a bad event never happened. Feelings of sadness and regret disappear for a while, but when the mind-numbing substance is removed, natural emotions can be difficult to manage.

"My life is a swirling vortex of emotion," a recovering alcoholic quipped as he smiled through the pain. He'd managed his emotions with alcohol for 50 years. In counseling, we talked about putting bad feelings into words rather than lashing out in anger or getting drunk again.

"I got a bad feeling in my brain," complained an older gentleman who had fallen into a habit with pain medication. This rather lame way of describing his anger was the best he could do. He needed someone to talk to. He needed some help putting feelings into words.

Emotional swirls of early recovery can be hard on relationships. Feelings once masked by substance abuse suddenly spew forth. A wife tells her husband how she truly feels. A husband talks about things unsaid for years.

Lisa covered up anger and depression with alcohol. She had problems with her boss but rarely told him how she truly felt. She worked through lunch, stayed late in the office, and gave up vacation time. She didn't complain or say no. She did all she could to meet his unreasonable demands, but her efforts were ignored and her contributions criticized. She felt overwhelmed by suppressed emotion, so she stopped by the liquor store on her way home. That became a habit.

A nervous breakdown led her to my office. We talked about the depression–addiction connection. She stopped drinking, joined AA, and started counseling. We talked about setting limits, and she learned how to say no to unreasonable demands. She left the office at five o'clock, and she didn't take work home. She carved out some time in her schedule for the things she liked to do. Anger became easier to manage. Alcohol was replaced by verbal expressions of emotion and healthier ways to relax.

Her healthy new choices came with unexpected results. Standing up for herself and tactfully expressing her opinion led to duty changes at work. She got a new boss. He recognized her value and rewarded her assertiveness (and sobriety). She was promoted and given a raise.

Worst-moment recall. When people ask for help stopping addiction, I often ask them to focus on the worst moments they can recall that are connected to doing the bad thing. Those worst moments are often times of embarrassment in front of other people or shame in private moments. For one person, the worst moment may include being handcuffed by police. For another, it may be getting sick of herself while sitting on the edge of a bed. Worst-moment recall can be a catalyst for change. Early in substance-abuse counseling, I usually ask,

"When were you the most sick of yourself and your habit?"

"How did it feel?"

"Where were you sitting?"

"What did the room look like?"

"Who was there?"

"Do you remember the smell...the sounds...the way the couch (chair, floor) felt?"

Recall of these memories usually brings back the emotion of that moment and impetus to change. People in AA call this "keeping it green." I call it common sense—learning from mistakes of the past.

Medication Tools

The National Institute on Alcohol Abuse and Alcoholism (NIAAA) recommends medication treatment of addiction when people are unable to stop the bad habit on their own.[6] The benefits of these medications, however, are very limited, and they should be combined with counseling support.

Some medications reduce cravings. Others reduce the pleasure effects of abusing a substance. *Acamprosate* (Campral) reduces cravings for alcohol. *Naltrexone* (ReVia, Depade) reduces alcohol's mood-elevating effects. These medications offer modest help for a patient who's already motivated to recover.

One medication works by creating fear of drinking. *Disulfiram* (Antabuse) causes vomiting if someone drinks alcohol while taking it. Fear of vomiting helps keep a patient sober. Again, this medication works best in a motivated patient.

Margaret, a middle-aged lawyer, told me how she used disulfiram to get through her early months of sobriety. When she woke up in the morning, she felt good and didn't want a drink. She was happy to wake up without a hangover. She took the medication with breakfast and felt good about her choice. As courtroom stress chipped away at her peace of mind, she began to think about having a drink. By five o'clock, in the middle of frustrating traffic jams, she would regret her choice and curse the medication. She wanted to block out her bad feelings, but she didn't drink because she knew the medication would make her sick. By the next morning she was once again grateful for her sobriety and would take another tablet.

The most important role for medication in alcoholism is in detoxification. Heavy drinkers who stop alcohol abruptly may develop seizures. Sedatives such as *diazepam* or *gabapentin* reduce the risk of seizures and delirium tremens. These medicines are usually prescribed in hospital detox settings.

Treatment of underlying illness. This is where medications really help. It can be hard to stay sober if your brain is chemically unbalanced by black moods. Depression may lead to addiction, and addiction to depression. It's a frustrating loop. To stop either one, you should deal with both.

Medications help break the depression–addiction connection. Antidepressants can reduce feelings of futility and irritability that may lead to a first drink. Successful treatment empowers people to think and feel clearly so they can benefit from counseling and group support.

To fully benefit from antidepressants, the addict must stop the bad habit. A middle-aged housewife told me, "I can feel the alcohol just suck the goodness right out of the medication." It was a colorful illustration of the medication-blocking effects of substance abuse. Avoiding the wrong chemicals and finding the right ones is part of the recovery process.

Other people worry about trading addiction to alcohol for addiction to medication. A middle-school teacher asked, "Are antidepressants habit-forming?" The answer is no. Antidepressant medications are not addicting. Nobody "gets high" on antidepressants. When treatment is complete, they are usually quite easy to stop.

Dependence on antidepressants is more like dependence on high blood pressure medicine than dependence on alcohol. If you stop blood pressure medicine too early, blood pressure problems come back. If you stop antidepressants too soon, black moods will return.

Inpatient rehabilitation. Some people need to be separated from temptation to get recovery started. They need a "time-out." Residential programs offer a place to eat, sleep, and learn about sobriety through group and individual counseling. People begin to realize they're not alone in their struggles. Group support helps.

Most programs last for 28 days or longer. One month in rehab gives the brain time to recover from alcohol damage. Better brain function usually leads to clearer thinking and better choices.

Twenty-eight days of clean living may also relieve symptoms of depression. Most people are quite depressed on the day they arrive for treatment. These dark moods often resolve themselves without antidepressant treatment before they leave. If oppressive sadness continues, medication should be started and continued during outpatient treatment

Use the Tools

Recovery from addiction is a process. Like keeping a nice garden, sprouts of bad habits must be uprooted again and again. The handful of tools suggested in this chapter will help.

The "shovel of faith" can help. Give the problem to God. Give it to Him again. Then give it to Him again. Be willing to let God change your heart, empowering you to let go of pleasures that don't come through Him. Ask Him, every day, to not lead you into temptation and deliver you from evil.

The "boot of behavior" can help. Stomp down the weeds. Say no again and again. When temptations sprout from everyday events, step away. Move away from the people and places that lead to bad choices. Walk into a place where an accountability group is meeting.

Medical tools can help, especially if depression and addiction are growing together. Treatment of underlying depression removes the seeds of weeks and potentials for bad habits. Recovery from depression brings vitality. This new way of experiencing life can be focused on the recovery process.

It's good to look over a garden and see flowers in a place where weeds once grew. It will also be good to look over your day and see healthy choices where addictions once dominated.

Action Items

1. Make a commitment to stop a bad habit.
2. Seek your Higher Power.
3. Stay away from the people and places that feed your bad habit.
4. Throw away the stuff that leads you up the ladder and down the slope.
5. Understand that early weeks of renewal may involve craving, sleep problems, and physical aches.
6. Don't forget the worst moments of your bad habit.
7. Use the building blocks of HALT to help construct a wall of self-control.
8. Find some people to support your new healthy choices. Get to know them.
9. Recognize recovery as a process of replacing bad habits with good ones.
10. As good things begin to happen, develop a grateful heart.

Chapter 14

Medicate Chemical Imbalances

*"Jesus said, 'It is not the healthy who need a
doctor, but the sick.'"*

MATTHEW 9:12

Sometimes we need a medical doctor. Sometimes we need a coach. Consider this chapter to be your medication coach. It can't substitute for the guidance of a caring physician, but it outlines a plan for restored brain fitness. It anticipates obstacles and will help you to stay focused on the goal—the return of your abilities to love and to work. So...

"Run faster!"

"You can do it!"

"Get out there and do your best!"

Sports coaches lead athletes to success by encouraging them along a program of physical conditioning and mental focus. A doctor can do the same for a patient by outlining a plan for victory over black moods and giving support through that process.

The second SMART step of renewal is to medicate the chemical imbalance. For people with disabling periods of sadness, rebalance of brain chemistry can be a life-changing step. If you've been deeply depressed for more than two weeks, consider Step M. If black moods are impairing your abilities to love and to work, consider Step M. If your depressive moods don't go this low, then you may be able to skip to step A—adjustment of your expectations. However, if you ignore the recommendations of Steps S and M when problems are present in these areas, then subsequent steps will be less effective.

Before Starting Medication

For periods of mild depression, don't jump to medications too quickly. First, do the things you know can be helpful. Pray. Read the Bible. Read books that express Christian viewpoints on recovery from depression. Increase your exercise to blow off daily stress. Cut back on excessive responsibilities. If these don't help, consider professional counseling. Then, if these nonmedical helps don't get you back on your feet, talk to a doctor about medications.

An excellent example of healthy stress management that failed to overcome black moods comes from the experiences of a women's ministry leader. Beth jogged on the treadmill for 30 minutes each day. She danced with a jazzercise class every Tuesday. She retreated to a cabin in the woods when she needed to relax. She prayed at her church twice each week and meditated quietly by herself for an hour every day. When these healthy choices failed, she began seeing a therapist.

Despite doing all the right things, her moods continued to darken and her sense of closeness to God began to disappear. It took a little time for her to realize that her depression needed medical treatment. She had referred others for medical help. Now it was time to refer herself.

Beth began using antidepressant medication. She needed a little coaching at first. Some early problems with nausea made her think about stopping. Medical coaching kept her focused on the goal—return of her spiritual vitality. With slow changes in dosage and patience, Beth beat the black moods. Her spiritual joy returned as her oppressive darkness disappeared. She began dancing with life again.

Before trying medication, pray, exercise, and seek good counsel—but don't wait too long before talking to a doctor. If you wait until loved ones leave or you get fired from a job, then you've waited too long. While antidepressants can still help at this point, you and your loved ones may go through needless suffering.

Get Past the Excuses

It's time to get off of the bench. There are plenty of excuses for not considering medication. Don't let those excuses keep you sidelined. Feeling personally or spiritually weak are not good excuses. Too often I hear the words "I should be able to do this myself." As if a little more motivation could reverse their brain problem, people try praying more, exercising more, and eating better diets. These are rarely enough to cure black moods. So they sit on the sidelines with their sadness.

At our first meetings, I see worry rise in the eyes of some patients as we approach the topic of medication. They feel weak and embarrassed for even considering the idea.

A national-security agent brought this dilemma to my office. As a political historian, he knew about world leaders who had battled depression. As a Christian, he knew of biblical references to finding virtue through hardship. He was mad at himself for not beating depression on his own. As we saw, Abraham Lincoln didn't take medication. Neither did King David or Martin Luther. They simply endured the darkness until it ran its course. Untreated, this affliction can last for years.

The agent didn't have time to wait. He was missing days at work and at risk of losing his job. When I suggested medication, his eyes filled with worry. What if his supervisors found out? He was worried how this visit to my office might affect his security clearance and career. How could he reconcile his use of medication with his beliefs about spiritual growth through suffering? He needed some coaching to get over the obstacles of feeling personally and spiritually weak.

Rather than focusing on the word *depression,* I encouraged him to focus on his problems with insomnia, irritability, and poor concentration. Loss of sleep, he understood, was making it hard to focus on his work and remain patient with his family. I reminded him that sleep deprivation has been used to coerce prisoners of war to reveal intelligence information. It impairs good judgment and decision making and leads to a painful state of mind.

Seeing his condition as a collection of brain impairments helped him to get past the stigma he associated with the word *depression*. After two weeks of sleep medication (antidepressant), he was able to return to full function at work and loving involvement with his family.

Others feel that use of mood medication implies spiritual weakness. One of my spiritually minded patients refused to start medication because she believed it was "not of God." Another felt compelled to "pray the evil off" the tablets. She took the medication for a few days, but spiritual embarrassment took over. She stopped antidepressants and returned to her prayers for supernatural healing. Most likely, she's still on the sidelines with depression—crippled by worry, isolated from her family and friends at church.

A popular story about prayer may be helpful at this point. A man was stuck on a deserted island. Day after day, he prayed for God to send an airplane to rescue him. He prayed faithfully, fasted, and waited for a plane. One day, God sent a boat. The captain of the vessel invited him on board. This wasn't the rescue the man had in mind, so he didn't get on the boat. He remained stranded on the lonely island, waiting for a plane.

As a medication coach, I challenge my patients to "get in the boat"— to see God's involvement in medicine. Sometimes God sends instant healing from above. More often He sends a slow-moving boat. If you suffer from black moods, pray for the instant miracle, but don't miss the boat.

If you wonder about the spiritual rightness or wrongness of using medication to change your mood, I encourage you to focus on the fruits. If medication use is a spiritual weakness, it will lead to separation from God and His way. If medication use is right with God, it will lead to spiritual fruits. If correction of brain-cell dysfunction leads to more vital Christian work, then let the fruits speak for themselves.

Remember that depression can be a problem with the brain. Like avoiding stroke or heart attack through the use of high blood pressure medication—like avoiding blindness and amputation by treating diabetes with insulin—treating depression with antidepressants may yield good fruit, restoring relationships, job performance, and spiritual joy.

Get Back in the Game

An overwhelmed accountant came to my office after worries about work reassignments became too much to handle. Betty hadn't been to work in two weeks and could no longer keep up with care for her children. She sat in the chair beside me, rapidly emptying a box of Kleenex. I empathized with her struggle and reassured her that things would get better. Then I suggested counseling and medical treatment.

She became visibly angry and insisted I must be wrong. Moving to the edge of her seat and leaning forward, she pleaded, then firmly demanded, "There must be another way! I do *not* need medication!"

We discussed her problems and treatment options, again and again. Each time, I reminded Betty that in cases of severe depression the best course of treatment includes antidepressant medication. Her irrational anger and circular arguments became frustrating to me. She had stayed longer than usual, and I knew that my next patient was waiting. She demanded my help but rejected my advice.

Finally, a little annoyed, I looked her squarely in the eye, raised the tone of my voice, and sternly insisted she must make a decision. I said, "You can take medication and get better, or not take medication and stay the way you are. There is no third choice!"

She left my office with a prescription in hand, a little angry and surprised that a Christian doctor could be so seemingly harsh. She came back to my office three weeks later with a big smile on her face and a blueberry pound cake in her hands. The cake was delicious. Betty was back in the game!

Like an athlete in a game of basketball, sometimes we need a swift kick of motivation to get us moving in the right direction. Sometimes we need a medication coach to firmly state the best course for tomorrow. Sometimes we just need to trust and submit to God-given coaches.

Recovery from injury

In many ways, medications function like a cast around a broken bone. Stabilizing a bone with a cast allows other healing mechanisms to function. In a similar way, stabilizing the brain with medication allows the healing effects of counseling and spirituality to do their work. By stabilizing and realigning broken parts of the brain, antidepressants enable people to think more clearly in counseling and more fully experience spiritual joy.

For short-term depression, medications provide a temporary cast, a stabilized environment for healing to take place. Medications settle down an overwhelmed nervous system so that the brain's growth factors and repair functions can do their work. (Some of these self-repair processes were discussed in chapter 3.)

For longer periods of depression, longer periods of stabilization may be needed. For serious bone fractures, people need metal screws or steel plates to keep the bone stabilized for years. Likewise, with more serious forms of depression, longer-term stabilization with medications may be needed. A stabilized leg allows a man to enjoy a game of golf. A stabilized brain enables him to enjoy his family, his job, and his God.

Restoring Brain Fitness

Competitive swimmers often visualize a point of success as they train. In a similar way, it helps people in black moods to focus on a day of renewal. In depressive darkness, the main goals are to restore your abilities to love and to work. Antidepressants don't eliminate bad moods or hard times. They are intended to restore your brain's natural mood balance and thinking abilities. This mind–body tune-up is aimed at restoring your brain's ability to function as God intended.

For you to understand the words you're reading on this page, specific circuits in your brain must be working just right. Slight imbalances in these circuits will slow down your reading speed and impair your ability to remember words. Major malfunctions in these chemical circuits will make it impossible. That's what happens to people in depression. Their abilities to think and feel normally become impaired by chemical imbalances. Sometimes counseling or the passage of time will correct these balances; other times a medication is needed.

After his recovery from major depression, an electrician compared his need for medication to adjustments on an old-fashioned television. Older televisions, he explained, had a large knob to make big changes in channel frequency and a smaller knob to do the fine-tuning. The big knob got the television near the right station, and the small knob brought the picture into focus.

"My seeking healing through counseling alone," he suggested, "was like adjusting the fine-tuning knob when major adjustments were needed." It made sense to seek counseling for conflicts with co-workers. It made sense to work on improving stress management. But these fine adjustments did not come close to relieving his black moods. He needed a major adjustment to his brain chemistry. After adjusting the big "medication knob," the little "counseling knob" worked a lot better. Together, medication and counseling brought things back into focus.

The goal of medication treatment is not a cosmetic alteration of mood but a correction of imbalance that leads to renewal of vitality. Medication should improve your ability to handle stress, stop the chemical cascade, and restore your brain's healthy operation. The ultimate goal of medical treatment is to restore your ability to enjoy your work and loved ones.

Getting Started

When it's time to begin medication a good basic principle is, *Start low and go slow.* To reduce the possibility of side effects, think about starting with a lower dose than the one suggested by manufacturers. Increase the dose every few days to the recommended dose if side effects do not become a problem. Do not exceed the doses recommended by your doctor. Like any medication, a little antidepressant is a good thing; too much is not. Take each of these steps under the guidance of a coaching physician. Don't substitute the suggestions of any book (including this one) for a careful discussion with your doctor.

First-week goals. Antidepressants take two to four weeks to relieve black moods. Sometimes people need more immediate help. In these cases, short-term use of a second medication may be a good idea.

Getting a good night of sleep is often a first goal of medication management. Depression can make it hard to sleep. People struggle to stay asleep at night, then fight to stay awake in the day. It's a mess. The brain was not created to work in this way. Lack of rest leads to brain-cell dysfunction, fuzzy thinking, and frazzled emotions. A snowball effect often follows—depression leads to insomnia and sleep deprivation leads to deeper depression.

It's good to sleep when it is dark outside and to be awake when it's light. It's the way our bodies were designed to work. The simplicity of this truth may get lost during the emotional upheaval of black moods.

When I meet a stressed-out individual who can't sleep, I focus on getting him a good night of rest. First we talk about good sleep habits: reduce caffeine, keep a consistent schedule, and increase exercise in the daytime. If simple steps do not help, I may suggest medication. Sleep is a relatively easy thing to fix—a little clonazepam, trazodone, or zolpidem can create an irresistible urge to go to sleep.

Being unconscious for eight hours in the middle of the night works wonders. The world seems far less oppressive. It's easier to face problems the next day after a restorative evening of rest. Using medication for sleep is often a short-term solution. It can usually be stopped after a few weeks—when the antidepressant begins to work.

A second early goal for medical treatment is to reduce a patient's level of daytime worry. Black moods come with gnawing anxiety. People worry too much. Unhealthy levels of stress hormones trigger the chemical cascade and depression gets deeper. Antidepressants will get rid of this worry in a few weeks, but sometimes people need help to get through a crisis. Short-term use of an anxiety-reducing medication can help you stop overreacting to everyday nuisances. It can stop the snowball effect of more worry...more depression...more worry...more depression. A little clonazepam or lorazepam usually soothes the overactive brain cells so people can think more clearly and make better sense of their problems.

The dosage of anti-anxiety medication should be high enough to create calmness and a "can-do" feeling, but not so high as to cause sluggishness in speech and thinking. Since these short-term cures for anxiety may be habit forming, it's best to use them in small doses for just a few weeks.

First-month goals. It will take two to four weeks of daily antidepressants to beat most cases of depression. Be patient. Have a thoughtful discussion with your doctor in order to pick the right medication. Get started. Then wait.

Choosing which antidepressant to use depends on which symptoms are causing you the most trouble. All antidepressants can be helpful in depression. Some are better for insomnia. Others are better for low energy. The table below lists some of the most popular antidepressants and the symptoms they're most uniquely suited to treat.

If low energy and poor concentration mark your depression, a dopamine- or norepinephrine-enhancing medication may work the best. Bupropion is the only popular antidepressant that produces a big boost of dopamine activity. It is also the best choice for people who are highly concerned about weight gain or sexual side effects. Risks of sexual slowness and appetite stimulation are lowest with bupropion.

If your depression is marked by insomnia, *mirtazapine* may be a good choice. This medication induces sleep, has little effect on sex life, but has a significant risk of weight gain. The appetite stimulation of mirtazapine may be especially helpful to those who have lost a lot of weight as part of their mood illness.

In depression that is marked by excessive worry, a serotonin drug like *fluoxetine* or *escitalopram* may be most helpful. These serotonin medications also help to reduce the excessive self-criticism that may come with depression. It may be hard to believe that medication can reduce a person's tendency to criticize herself, but the serotonin antidepressants do it quite well. They have a way of breaking the cycle of going over and over and over the same problem. Breaking this obsessive cycle allows the mind to move on to other things.

The most common side effects of the serotonin antidepressants are diminished sexual interest and modest weight gain. Not everyone will develop these side effects, but among those who do, most people find that the good effects outweigh the bad.

Popular Antidepressants and Their Brain-Chemistry Actions
(Generic names in parentheses)

SRIs—Serotonin re-uptake inhibitors

Lexapro *(Escitalopram)*
Prozac *(Fluoxetine)*
Many others

SNRIs—Serotonin norepinephrine re-uptake inhibitors

Cymbalta *(Duloxetine)*
Pristiq *(Desvenlafaxine)*
Others

DNRIs—Dopamine norepinephrine re-uptake inhibitors

Wellbutrin *(Bupropion)*

All of the antidepressants work pretty well. None have been proven to always work any better than any of the others. One medication may be more helpful to you, while another is more helpful to your friend. As a group, antidepressants reduce symptoms in 60 to 70 percent of people who use them; 30 percent of patients show little or no improvement. These folks will need to change medication or try another method of treatment.

Most people do quite well on generic forms of antidepressants. People usually notice little difference between generic and brand-name products. One exception may be the sustained release (SR) and extended release (XL) generic formulations of *bupropion*, some of which appear to be less effective for the patients in my practice. Otherwise, generics usually provide an economical alternative for many people who need lower-cost medication. The figure below lists a few generic antidepressants and their distinguishing benefits.

Special Target Symptoms of Antidepressants (Generic)	
Medication	*Especially helpful with…*
Bupropion	Low energy
Doxepin	Stomach and bowel irritability
Fluoxetine	Excessive worry
Mirtazepine	Sleep and weight loss
Nortriptyline	Headaches

Finding the right antidepressant may take some time. There are no blood tests or brain scans to match your specific depressive symptoms to the best medication. Finding the right medication comes through trial and error. Start by identifying the main target symptoms you want to hit and the main side effects you most want to avoid. Many people get better on the first try. Others need several medication attempts and more patience. It may take two to three trials, each lasting two to four weeks, to find the right antidepressant for you.

The Long-Term Game Plan

An athlete who wants to run marathons doesn't stop training after finally making it 26 miles. He keeps running on a daily basis to stay in shape. If you want to remain free of black moods, don't stop medications because the symptoms are gone.

If they are helping, continue antidepressants for at least six months. For people with a long history of depression, medications may be needed for much longer. Dosages can sometimes be reduced with long-term use. Others may need higher doses or a medication switch during long-term use.

Olympic medalist Dennis Adkins had to learn the importance of staying on medication the hard way. For many years before his Olympic victory, Adkins struggled with periods of black moods. He coped with the sadness by running track, reading the Bible, and praying. Eventually, the illness led to severe insomnia and a 17-pound weight loss. He decided it was time for medical help. He found a doctor and began using antidepressants. Black-mood symptoms disappeared. Adkins felt pretty good, so he stopped medication.

He won an Olympic gold medal for running the 400-meter hurdles in world record time but soon became depressed again. This time he considered suicide. Even the joy of gold-medal success couldn't keep the chemicals balanced in his brain. So he restarted medication and found relief, again. Adkins went on to say, "Winning the Olympics was a great victory, but overcoming my depression was an even greater one."[1]

Long-term use of medication may be necessary to ensure long-term recovery. If you were depressed for a long time before medication, you'll probably need medication for longer than six months. For those who need medications for several years, the dosage or type of antidepressant may need some adjustment. "Prozac poop-out," an endearing phrase used by many psychiatrists, refers to the loss of effect that sometimes occurs with long-term antidepressant use. It can usually be remedied by increasing the dose.

Doses of medications can be adjusted up or down based on symptoms. For some people, doses may be adjusted based on the level of irritability. For others, problems with sleep determine how much medication is enough.

The bingo indicator

For one older woman, bingo was the indicator. I could have reliably adjusted her dose of medication by asking how many times she'd played bingo in the past month. One of the first signs that Mrs. Carter was slipping into depression was her withdrawal from her bingo-playing friends. Frequent bingo signified that she was also doing well with the rest of her life. Little bingo signified a need for more medication. Clearly, treating her depression was more complicated than monitoring her bingo activity. However, not treating the depression that interfered with her enjoyment of life would have led to deeper black moods. Her depression remained in long-term remission with medication.

Few people like the idea of long-term medication. I don't like the fact I will probably need anticholesterol medication for the rest of my life. To keep my cholesterol balanced and reduce the risk of stroke, I'll do it. If you suffer with chronic black moods, you'll face a similar choice. Take medication to restore brain cell function, or risk damage to your loving and working relationships.

Leaping Hurdles—Side-Effect Management

For some people, beating depression with medication is more like getting through an obstacle course than running a marathon. Most people experience minimal side effects from antidepressants. Others face annoying obstacles.

Side effects usually show up first, and good effects show up later. This may create a bad initial impression of what medication can do. When people experience nausea or dry mouth without the benefit of mood elevation, they frequently give up. To experience what antidepressants can do, continue the effort for at least six weeks. This will allow time for most side effects to resolve and the helpful effects to become clear. If the medications are working, stay with the brain-fitness program for another six months under the guidance of a coaching physician.

The *Physicians' Desk Reference* is a seven-pound book of lists.[2] It describes over 50 possible side effects for most medications. Few of these problems ever occur. However, when they do, they become obstacles on your path to renewal. Most side effects go away with time. Push your way through them. Others make it necessary for you to stop one medication and try another. Move around the obstacle. Be persistent. Reasonable and hopeful treatment of depression means watching for side effects but keeping your eyes on the goal of black-mood break-through.

Nausea and sedation are the most common short-term side effects of antidepressants. Don't let them keep you from your goal. Nausea almost always goes away in a few days. Sedation can often be over-come by moving the medication to bedtime.

Weight gain and decreased sexual function are two common long-term side effects. The wife of one of my patients complained, "He's become like my friend. He lost that spark in his eye…and that's not good." If you lose your interest in sex, consider a change to bupropion. It rarely effects sexual function. If you are concerned about weight gain, avoid mirtazepine. It can add inches to your waistline in weeks. A doctor who knows about these side effects can coach you around the obstacles.

Sometimes, antidepressants result in too much control of mood. This isn't good either. In getting rid of depressed feelings, antidepres-sants sometimes create a flat mood. Some people miss their feelings of sadness and anger. After three months on medication a dentist came back to my office complaining that she was the only one not crying at a funeral. A restaurant manager who used anger to motivate his employees complained that he no longer felt like yelling at his staff. Rather than discuss other ways to manage his employees, he stopped medication, ended therapy, and became angry again.

The goal we're aiming for is to get rid of disabling sadness without flattening mood. Antidepressant medications should keep low moods from getting too low, not make people feel "emotionally neutered." With dosage adjustment or change in medication, this can usually be done.

Other people get *too much* emotion as a side effect. In lifting the mood out of depression, medications have a small risk of creating manic excitement. Some people are exquisitely sensitive to the activating effects of antidepressants. They lose sleep, talk too fast, and make impulsive decisions. This manic excitement can cause just as many problems as deep depression. Mania often leads to impulsive behaviors that people later regret. Watching for overshoot of mood recovery is most important in bipolar types of depression.

Finally, a rare but serious side effect risk can be an increase in suicidal thinking. Thoughts about wishing to be dead are common in a state of deep depression. Thoughts of suicide are not uncommon. Some research shows increased risk for thoughts of suicide in children and adolescents taking antidepressants. Other studies find no such change. This uncommon but potentially serious risk calls for watchful eyes from families and physicians, especially in the early weeks of treatment. If depression gets worse instead of better, call the prescribing doctor. Medication may need to be adjusted or stopped.

Still, one thing is clear—antidepressants provide a lifesaving help to many children and adults with black moods. Not treating deep depression with medication has its own risks of self-destructive behaviors. Watch for the risks—but keep your eyes on the goal.

An Intimidating Opponent—Hard-to-Manage Depression

Although many people find relief with the first medication, some do not. First, second, and third attempts may fail. This is when you really need an experienced medication coach. You wouldn't use a high school football coach to prepare for a college bowl game. You shouldn't rely on your family doctor to treat more challenging periods of depression.

Too many people wait until they lose their jobs or loving relationships before they switch from a general practitioner to a psychiatrist. A defeated computer saleswoman came to my office last month after failing to get better under the care of her family doctor. She laid a two-page list of unmet performance objectives on my desk. Her boss was preparing to let her go. Treatment-resistant depression had caused her performance to deteriorate. We found a new combination of medications to soothe her excess worry and restore her positive outlook, but these steps came too late to save her job.

When common strategies don't work, you may need to get creative. One such approach is to combine different types of antidepressants. A landmark study recently completed by the National Institutes of Mental Health, called the Sequenced Treatment Alternatives to Relieve Depression (STAR*D) study,[3] found that switching or combining antidepressants lead to a recovery rate of 70 percent.

Very often, a little of this medication and a little of that medication can produce the desired effect—sometimes with fewer side effects than big doses of one antidepressant. There is little scientific evidence to guide these choices, so they depend on the experience of your psychiatrist.

One very effective combination of medication is using a serotonin-enhancing antidepressant (for example, fluoxetine) along with one that boosts the level of dopamine (for example, bupropion). This combination brings together the benefits of dopamine enhancement (energy and concentration) and the benefits of serotonin rebalance (calmness and reduced worry). There are many other combinations that also work well.

Another strategy for beating hard-to-manage depression is the off-label use of medicines. "Off-label" means that the medications are not approved by the FDA for use in depression. Even so, in research studies or clinical experience, these medications have been found to be useful. Two common off-label strategies include the use of sedating medications such as quetiapine and the use of hormone augmentation with thyroxin. These augmenting medications can be used along with standard antidepressants to enhance their mood-elevating effects.

If medication efforts fail, it may be time for stronger measures. ECT (electroconvulsive therapy) or shock therapy has been shown to be more effective than medication in treatment of resistant depression. Newer technologies include transcranial magnetic stimulation (TMS) and vagal-nerve stimulation (VNS). These newer depression treatments need more study but offer hope to those with difficult-to-treat black moods.

Winding Down the Fitness Program—Stopping Medication

If antidepressant medications are working, use them as long as you need them to control the black moods and to enjoy your life. They are not habit-forming and have minimal risks to your body. People use them for years without problems.

When you are ready to stop, have a little talk with your medication coach. For short-term depressive periods, medications can usually be stopped after six months. Loss of a loved one or getting released from a job may trigger short-term depression and require short-term use of medication. However, if you've been depressed for many years or most of your life, you may benefit from long-term medical treatment.

Some antidepressants need to be discontinued very slowly. Stopping paroxetine or venlafaxine too quickly can produce a flu-like syndrome of body aches and peculiar physical sensations. In general, it is best to stop brain medications slowly. Decease the dose by half for a few weeks, and then decrease by one half again before stopping. If the underlying chemical imbalance is still present, you will see the symptoms of black moods return.

Roslyn has needed to use two medications for several years. Every few years, we try to reduce the dose of one medication to see if she still needs it. Recently, we tried to reduce the dose of one medication by one half. The outcome was bad. She came back to my office one week later in a state of suicidal depression. The night before our appointment, she had put a bottle of pills into her mouth and then spit them in the sink. We restarted her usual dose of medicine, and her mood quickly recovered.

Not all relapses will occur with this speed. It may take days to months for the underlying chemical imbalance to show itself. Like high-blood-pressure medications, antidepressants treat a symptom—not the root cause. If you stop either medication too early, your high blood pressure will return, or your black moods will resurface.

On the other hand, if the underlying chemical imbalance has been settled, you will no longer need the medication. Like recovery from diabetes, lifestyle changes and time may allow the body to heal—no longer needing medical help.

Brigitte came to my office with deep depression and thoughts of driving her little pickup truck into a bridge embankment. She needed one medication to break her depression and another to get some sleep.

After several weeks, we stopped the sleep medication without problems. Over the next year, she reduced her academic load and found a new group of friends. Her mood remained stable, so we gradually stopped the antidepressant. She has been doing very well for many years. I see her mother once in a while. She tells me that Brigitte is doing fine, working as a waitress and happily married.

Even after several years, depression can come back. Once you have ended treatment, it's important to watch for signs of recurrence. After one depressive episode, the symptoms are easier to recognize. This awareness can lead you to earlier treatment and prevent the problems from becoming so intense the next time.

Teamwork. For many people, deciding when to stop medications is best handled as a team decision between patient, doctor, and a concerned loved one. For people battling depression without a supportive family member or friend, a counselor/therapist can be a valuable member of the team. While individual patients make most decisions about starting and stopping medication, including a third person in the decision can be quite helpful.

In this three-person partnership, the opinion of each person is highly valued. Clearly, the experience of the doctor should take precedence when depression impairments are clear; but at times when the symptoms are not so obvious, a three-part team can be quite helpful in making these choices.

If any member of the team has good reason for the patient to stay on medication, it should probably be continued. A spouse, for example, may see signs of depression that a patient or doctor may not. A close friend or family member may note social isolation. A therapist may note problems with irritability. I learn a lot from the insights of family members and therapists. The patient benefits from treatment that's based on three points of view.

A Word About Natural Remedies

Many people are drawn to natural remedies for illness. The term *natural remedy* sounds comfortable and safe, like a walk in the park—refreshing. Natural products are usually chemicals derived from plants, then refined and concentrated in tablets. These chemicals extracted from plants seem safer than chemicals engineered by man. This is not always true.

Digitalis, which comes from the foxglove flower, is a common medication used to control irregular heart rates. This chemical extracted from a flower is highly fatal if the dose gets too high. Natural remedies are not always safe. If they're producing desirable changes in body chemistry, they may also have risks of undesirable changes (that is, side effects).

Others are drawn to natural cures because they want to avoid being known as someone who takes psychiatric medication. They seek antidepressant effects without the antidepressant name. Some are embarrassed that relatives will find out. Others fear losing their jobs.

Washington, DC, has many top-secret jobs. Many of my patients have worked in these jobs and have worried about what their employers might think about psychiatric treatment. They are concerned about losing their security clearances. To avoid antidepressants, they have asked for help using natural remedies. Most have noticed little improvement. A few have placed their mental well-being above job concerns and switched to antidepressant medication. To the best of my knowledge, none of these patients have lost their security clearances or jobs. They've become more effective at work and more involved in their families.

Generally speaking, the natural remedies produce modest good effects and modest side effects. Saint-John's-wort, SAMe, and light therapy are three of the most popular natural remedies. Saint-John's-wort may work as well as antidepressant medication for mild depression, but it also interacts with oral contraceptive medications. SAMe has some research to support its use, but requires a large daily quantity of the compound to produce an effect. Light therapy is actually quite helpful in seasonal (fall-to-winter) depression. Response is often seen within one week.

Many nonpharmacological treatments are moderately helpful, but unproven, in recovery from mild depression. Religion, exercise, and diet are each very helpful and have their advocates. Unfortunately, they will not be formally evaluated for effectiveness because scientific research costs money.

This is the dark side of traditional medicine. While Western medicine is respected for its reliance on scientific proof, most clinical research is funded and guided by pharmaceutical corporations. These drug companies will not pay to prove that a treatment works unless they can make money on the product. Corporations cannot patent nutrients, light, or religion. Therefore, scientific proof of their positive or negative effects will remain lacking. Use of most nonmedical treatments will be guided by collective experiences of what works for individuals or small groups.

Faith and Chemistry

God can heal depression. Sometimes His touch brings immediate relief. Sometimes He works through helping relationships of loved ones or professionals. Quite often, He uses a tablet. Keep your mind open to the ways God can help.

Christ used a remedy of spit and mud to heal a man from blindness (see John 9:6). He healed another by prescribing a bath in a river. Today, Christ still heals through combinations of nature and faith. In the right time and place, medication and faith work together as a modern-day miracle mud.

A mixture of medicine and faith brought miraculous renewal to a middle-aged waitress named Mary. Seven years of depression had left Mary frustrated with the workings of her own mind and wishing to be dead. She'd sought help from counselors and tried several medications. She continued to pray for healing. Mary met a new counselor and tried a new medication. The antidepressant had a side effect of vivid dreaming. She hadn't been able to dream for years.

Mary's healing from depression came during a dream in the middle of the night. In this dream, her pastor was preaching a sermon on salvation. The pastor called her to the front of the sanctuary. He asked her to serve as a model for Christ's suffering, crucifixion, and resurrection. She walked to the front, where she modeled Christ's suffering and rebirth for the audience. Something miraculous happened at that moment. She awoke from the dream feeling "tingling and warmth from head to toe." Hopelessness and thoughts of suicide disappeared. She lay in a bed of spiritual contentment until morning. She stepped out of bed in a new state of mind. God used a combination of faith, chemistry, and a dream to heal her from the illness of dark moods.

Medicine and faith can work together. Few people will have a religious experience like the one experienced by Mary. More often, healing comes gradually as, day by day, people notice an improving sense of well-being. This gradual return to enjoyment of God's blessings and grace is no less miraculous than Mary's midnight miracle of healing. In God's time and in the way of His choosing, He can lead you to a black-mood breakthrough.

Action Items

1. Take a look at the checklist of depression symptoms in chapter 11. If you're experiencing three or more of the symptoms, consider asking a physician if antidepressant medication is advisable.
2. Before talking to a doctor:
    a. Think about what symptoms of depression interfere the most with your ability to love and to work.
    b. Ask someone among your family or friends to review the

chapter 11 checklist with you. Identify the symptoms they recognize in you.

3. Before accepting a medication from a doctor:

   a. Ask if the recommended prescription will help with the specific symptoms that are causing you trouble (for example, insomnia, irritability).

   b. Ask if the medication suggested is likely to cause side effects that you would most like to avoid (for example, weight gain or sexual slowness).

4. Be patient. Give the medication at least one month to work.

5. Remember that feeling better isn't a reason to stop using medication. It's often a sign the antidepressant is working.

6. If medication helps, continue using it for at least six months.

7. Consult your doctor before deciding to stop.

Chapter 15

Adjust Expectations of Yourself

*"In the morning I lay my requests before you
and wait in expectation."*

PSALM 5:3

Cars need fuel and electrical sparks to produce combustion. When these needs are met, the car moves down the road. Too much fuel and the engine will flood. Not enough spark and the engine will stall.

Emotions are like combustion. They depend on basic components. When basic needs for safety and self-worth are met, good moods can happen. When these needs aren't satisfied, emotions sputter along, imbalances occur, and an emotional tune-up is required.

Unmet Needs and Responses—Another Look

In chapter 6 several life stories illustrated the importance of meeting three basic needs: *safety, goodness,* and *power.* Exaggerated responses to these needs were discussed in terms of childhood vows and childhood resignations. Their roles in depression and recovery were highlighted.

In moderation, drives to ensure your safety and to feel good about yourself are healthy. In excess, they become exaggerated expectations that lead to personal turmoil and problems in relationships. Expectations

179

that are too high (vows) lead to frustration. Expectations that are too low (resignations) lead to giving up too easily. Both are pathways to dark moods.

In the chapter 6 world of unmet needs, Barbara's life story demonstrated the impact of childhood trauma on her expectations as an adult. She'd been abused by her father. Her mother stood by and did nothing. In the back of her mind, Barbara vowed that when she grew up she would never let anything bad happen to her children. It was an exaggerated childhood vow to ensure safety. She lived in fear. When the tragedy of September 11 happened in New York, she felt overwhelmed. It shattered her illusion that she could always protect her children. She became deeply depressed. Her recovery required that she lower her expectations.

Jim's life story illustrated the dangers of an excessive drive to prove goodness. His father had been harshly overcritical. Jim never felt good enough as a child or young adult. He struggled to prove his father wrong—he really was good enough. This deeply held passion became his unconscious childhood vow. It led him to musical and academic success in high school and college. He became an extraordinary success before the age of 30. Still, nothing satisfied. His exaggerated expectation of praise led him to frustration and depression. He lost touch with reality and was hospitalized. His recovery from depression depended on lowering his expectations.

The phrase "adjusting expectations" will be used quite often in this chapter. It's a shorthand way of describing changes in our deeply held motivations. In recovery from depression, some expectations must be lowered. Others must be raised.

As people pull into my office for emotional tune-ups, I look for unrealistic expectations about meeting basic needs. Some people react too strongly, trying to make the world safe or prove themselves good. Others give up too easily, expecting to be hurt or criticized or rejected again. Step A (adjust expectations) of SMART recovery begins with recognizing unhealthy expectations and ends with healthier ways to satisfy basic needs.

Basic Emotional Need #1: Safety

Feeling safe is our most basic emotional need. Without a sense of safety, all other emotional growth is stunted. Children who grow up in homes that violate a sense of safety learn to live in fear. They develop an emotional posture of being "on guard" in order to prevent further injury.

Children who are physically or sexually abused learn to be acutely careful of what they say and do. They learn that failing to recognize signs of intimidation may result in being violated again. On some level, we all learn to watch out, to scan our surroundings. We examine the facial expressions of others, check locks on doors, and sleep a little more lightly in strange surroundings. However, when people stay in this state of high alert, when they are unable to give rest to those fears—that's when emotional problems develop. Fear releases stress hormones. High levels of these hormones damage the heart, gut, and brain. Damage to brain cells may lead to depression. Part of their recovery is regaining a day-by-day sense of security.

Responses to Need for Safety		
	Vow	*Resignation*
Unhealthy Expectation	• I won't be hurt again	• Others will hurt me
Problems Created	• Fight or flight • Intrusiveness	• Passivity • Social retreat
Adjustments (Solutions)	• Lower expectations • Relax defensiveness	• Raise expectations • Exercise assertiveness
Healthy Expectation	"Generally secure"	

Safety vows. Some people react too strongly to concerns about safety. They make vows to themselves, consciously or unconsciously, that they will never be harmed again. They become hyper-vigilant—keeping body systems pumped up to maintain a high level of alertness. They expect bad things to happen. The fight-or-flight response is helpful if you meet a bear in the woods. It's harmful if you continuously live in that state of arousal.

Expecting that danger is imminent leads to problems in relationships. A woman guarding against another sexual assault may overreact in fear to a hug. This leads to turmoil inside. One emotion leads her to seek comfort in human touch, and another warns her to retreat in fear. Likewise, a man who is unconsciously guarding against another beating from his father may greet strangers with anger in his eyes. A similar conflict brews in his mind. One desire calls him to make a new friend. Another warns him not to be vulnerable. Both individuals live in fear and isolation, increasing the risk for black moods.

Parents who live with this expectation develop a heightened sense of responsibility to protect loved ones. They become overprotective, imagining dangers that do not exist. They regard the trusting attitudes of others as uniformed and unaware, and inadvertently teach children to feel unsafe themselves.

I see many mothers with depression. Of those who have grown up in homes with physical or emotional abuse, many have developed a habit of social withdrawal. It seems natural to teach children this way of avoiding emotional injury, even when there is no significant threat today. For parents caught up in this mind-set, recovery from black moods includes adjusting expectations about risks their children face in hallways at school or during an overnight stay at the home of a friend.

In one's spiritual life, holding on to this vow to make the world safe leads such a person to "get ahead" of God. A sense of urgency impels them to act now—and consult God later. For the spiritually minded person, developing healthier expectations means recognizing God's power to protect and provide comfort. Recalling an eternal perspective of God's plan for security helps soothe wounds of the past and offer hope for the future.

Sacrificing worry

In chapter 6, Barbara was frustrated and depressed by her need to make the world safe. After the events described in that chapter, her grandson developed cancer, and she became caught up in a mission to save him. She attended all doctor appointments, prayed for healing, and asked everyone she knew to do the same. Nothing she did brought her peace until she released his safety to God. As Abraham laid his son on an altar of sacrifice (Genesis 22:9), she laid her grandson on a mental altar of sacrifice. She regained her trust that God would do what's best. She continued to worry, but days of dark mood came around less often. Several months later, her grandson experienced his miracle.

In relationships, adjustments may need to be made in the way we look at our abilities and responsibilities. You are not a supermom or superdad. Sometimes your loved ones will be hurt. No level of worry will prevent it. Moderation of excessive responsibility is best for you and your loved ones. Step back. Allow your loved ones to make some choices about their safety. It will foster their sense of power and self-reliance.

Expecting positive outcomes tends to bring positive results. Expect that you'll be able to protect yourself. Expect to be able to enlist the help of protecting people. Relax your overactive imagination and learn to soothe yourself with expectations of safety and comfort.

Safety resignations.
   I am going to be hurt.
   Nothing I can do will prevent it.
   I might as well get used to it.
These are the thoughts of women and men resigned to the belief that they can't feel safe or secure. She feels fatigued. He feels burned out. They're paralyzed by fear of more pain. Expecting to be hurt justifies their social withdrawal. Expecting loved ones to fail convinces them, too, to give up. The world gets smaller as they retreat to their

corner of the house. In times like these, people give up on church and being together with other Christians. Prayers focus on surviving the next hour rather than victory through Christ.

Adjusting expectations of hurt and fear begins by changing our attitude in prayer. Expect God to change your resignation to *resolution*. Expect Him to create new feelings in your gut, and believe in His promises to protect you and your loved ones.

Trust one person—a spouse, a friend, or a counselor. Learning to trust one person makes it easier to trust another. Find a safe place to step out and risk. You can defend yourself and enlist others to help. Developing a sense of safety in one social setting makes it easier to step out in the next.

With both vows and resignations it's helpful to carefully calculate the real and imagined dangers. List your hardships of the past. Compare them to the actual dangers of today. Separating the emotional feelings of danger from the logical risks takes time. Renewing your mind rests on repeating healthy ways of thinking. Remind yourself—you really are quite safe today. Release those fears again tomorrow. The power of emotion to overpower clear thinking diminishes in the process.

Basic Emotional Need #2: Goodness

The need to feel good about ourselves is often regarded as less spiritual or noble than other aspirations. Feeling good about who you are may be looked at as selfish and unhealthy pride. Most counselors disagree. In the book *Search for Significance,* Christian counselor Robert McGee writes,

> Whether labeled "self-esteem" or "self-worth" the feeling of significance is crucial to man's emotional, spiritual, and social stability, and is the driving element within the human spirit. Understanding this single need opens the door to understanding our actions and attitudes.[1]

A healthy self-regard is critically important to maintaining healthy moods and fulfilling God's will in our lives. However, too much emphasis on personal goodness is a sign of emotional and spiritual illness. In *Happiness Is a Choice,* Christian psychiatrists Frank Minirth and Paul Meier write,

> Genuine self-worth is the opposite of false pride, which is a terrible sin committed primarily by individuals who are trying to compensate for their lack of self-worth.[2]

The psychological concept of self-worth overlaps with the spiritual concept of being right with God. A mental belief in self-worth, however, is not the same as this spiritual belief. A mental attitude of self-worth is more like a physical condition of fitness. Being physically fit has little to do with spiritual condition. You may be strong enough to run 20 miles but still not be right with God. Likewise, you may be emotionally strong in the area of self-worth, but again be out of step with God. Psychological self-worth has its roots in childhood experience. Spiritual rightness with God is rooted in acceptance of Christ's payment for our wrongdoing.

For the Christian, recognizing our relationship with God and the value He places on our lives should enhance our emotional fitness. It should bolster our self-esteem. Christ paid for your wrongs by His death on a bloody cross. That says a lot about your worth from an eternal perspective.

Roots of self-esteem. Our sense of self-worth is mostly learned in childhood. When children are harshly criticized throughout early years of their lives, they learn to feel "not good enough." As adults, they get stuck on thoughts about wrongs in their past—something from yesterday, last week, or years ago. Very often these thoughts are tucked away in the back of the mind (unconscious), quietly altering self-esteem and behavior. Such thoughts usually involve themes of disappointing loved ones. "I should have done better...I shouldn't have said that." People get stuck on beliefs that they aren't worthy of respect—not good enough.

When the only message children hear in childhood informs them that they aren't worthy of respect, some will resign themselves to that idea. Accepting this "fact" is an example of childhood resignation. It leads to a defeated mental attitude in adults.

Others, when faced with excessive criticism, will vow to prove themselves good. They will strive for perfection in order to prove the critics wrong. When such attempts become excessive, they may be called childhood vows. In adults, these vows lead to workaholic lifestyles and overcommitments. Puffed-up attitudes may lead to excessive sensitivity to criticism.

On the other hand, when children grow up with a balance of praise and criticism, they learn a sense of self-worth that empowers them to learn from and move on from criticism. As adults, they know that they're basically good people, able to rise above temporary feelings of inadequacy and shame. Part of recovery from depression is developing this mental attitude.

Responses to Need for a Sense of Goodness		
	Vow	*Resignation*
Unhealthy Expectation	• Must prove my value	• Will never gain approval
Problems Created	• Self-righteous • Easily offended	• Self-loathing • Reject praise
Adjustments (Solutions)	• Lower expectations • Depersonalize criticism	• Raise expectations • Focus on accomplishments
Healthy Expectation	"Good enough"	

Goodness vows. Recognizing that you're really quite good at something and attempting to prove that fact can be a healthy response to the need to feel good about yourself. It's a reasonable expectation. Some people will recognize your value. Others will not.

Expecting other people to consistently recognize your goodness leads to problems. For many, it's a sign of an unconscious vow to prove goodness. Those with an unmet need to feel good about themselves may overreact and present themselves as self-righteous. Ironically people who feel *not* good enough often demand that others act as if they *are*.

An unconscious vow to prove goodness gives rise to the thought, *Others must acknowledge my goodness or pay for their disrespect.* People who hold on to these unrealistic expectations cannot tolerate criticism. They get mad at other people who suggest they're wrong. They get mad at themselves when awareness of failure enters their minds. Such individuals strive to hide all bad things about themselves from others and, if possible, from themselves. Their internal monolog goes something like this:

Others shouldn't criticize me.

Others should speak of my greatness (even though I look down on myself).

People are waiting for me to fail. Then they will criticize.

Expecting to be criticized usually leads to criticism. Others get caught in this trap as normal disagreements become heated. This person is easily offended and, in turn, becomes offensive to others. Although he appears pompous and demanding on the outside, he feels "not good enough" in so many ways. Anger and biting remarks aren't far behind when this man's deeply held vow is challenged.

In areas of faith, the vow to prove goodness leads to expectations of special help from God. This brings disappointment with God for not providing the good feelings we think we must have. God seems oblivious to this deeply felt need.

From a spiritual perspective, there's no way to prove our goodness to God. For the Christian, goodness comes through Christ's payment for our wrongdoing. We're made good enough by His goodness, through turning to Him and receiving forgiveness. Whatever bad thing you've done can be forgiven. Yet deeply engrained memories fade slowly. It may be necessary to remind yourself of His forgiveness many times. Accept God's forgiveness, and trust that He has done what He promised to do in His Word. Hold on to the belief that "God loves me just as I am."

The psychological steps of adjusting expectations include reconsidering events of the past. Was the thing that you did really that bad? Was that thing someone did to you really that harmful? Reframing emotional memories in a more reasoned perspective can help. A friend or counselor may help you sort out the facts from emotionally charged memories.

The goal of adjusting expectations about self-worth is a healthy sense of goodness. I'm okay—acceptable as I am. I can tolerate the criticism of others. I can be wrong in this moment and still believe I'm a pretty good person.

A middle-aged graphic artist provides an example. She came to my office in a state of dark depression after being fired from her job. She had rarely said no to requests for extra tasks at work—forever searching for, but never finding, approval for a job well done. She was frustrated by failures to prove her value at work and at home. She was emotionally burned out. We traced the roots of her intense drive back to similar situations with her father. It started with childhood sibling rivalries and continued in conflicts as an adult.

I sat down with Rebecca and her father. She listed the ways she'd done well. He listed the ways she hadn't been good enough. As I watched them discuss these events, it felt more like a contest than a conversation. She and her father seemed to be working to make the other one look bad. Both had clear reasons to regret their past behaviors, but they found relief from that sense of badness by making the other one look morally wrong. Rebecca's vow to prove her own goodness was wearing her out.

Today, she's working to let go of her vow and step out of that vicious circle. She tries to do the right thing, offering respect to her father (and others) without overreacting when others don't do the same in return. She's learning to feel good about herself, independent of criticism, past or present.

Goodness resignations. Susan was referred to me by her family doctor for treatment of depression. Her story illustrates the value of confronting resignations. As we talked about her black-mood symptoms and low self-regard, a pattern of giving up too easily emerged. She'd been resigning herself to challenges since childhood. Harsh criticism and neglect had taught her that it was easier to accept disrespect than to stand up for herself.

As an adult, this low-value message continued. Under the guise of being helpful, her mother advised her that her husband would probably leave her for a more attractive woman. She advised her to leave him and come live with her. Whenever her phone would ring, Susan's pulse quickened, her stomach tightened, and her breathing became rapid. She was not able to pick up the receiver for fear of her mother's criticism. She became overwhelmed with worry and then with black moods.

In therapy, Susan is working to relearn the belief that she's a good person and that she has the power to stand up for herself. She's learning that her mother was wrong—that she *is* worthy of respect. Step by step, she's gently re-emerging in social circles with a more realistic belief in her goodness and her power to prove it. She's challenging the "helpful" criticisms of her mother and imposing reasonable limits on their phone conversations. She's satisfying the second core need.

Giving up on the need for self-worth leads to underachievement and social passivity. This resignation is fed by obsession on failures to please parents, teachers, and other loved ones. A belief that others will reject us may lead us to reject them first. An unhealthy pattern of thinking results: *Why bother trying if rejection is inevitable? Why defend my honor if I'll end up feeling bad again? It seems easier to give up now.*

Recognizing the good and the bad in our own behaviors is a sign of healthy self-regard. Getting stuck on the negative thoughts is not. When you consistently focus on the negative aspects of your behavior and expect others to do the same, the risk for depression increases. It becomes time for an adjustment of expectations.

In our spiritual lives, the image of God gets distorted by goodness resignations. Thinking patterns get sick, as reflected by thoughts such as…

God will let me down too.

He knows about my badness.

He'll reject me like the others. So why ask for more?

Instead of expecting rejection from God, consider His viewpoint. God's perspective on your value can replace self-critical impressions. God views you as forgiven—not perfect, but good enough. Slowly, this knowledge can change your distorted views of what God expects of you.

In relationships with others, learn to consider the source of criticism. Recognize that the words and behaviors of other people are just that—the opinions and deeds of people who have problems of their own. Early life lessons may have taught them that *they* weren't good enough. When they project their bad feelings onto you, don't accept them. Recognize that the source of some criticisms are based in the unmet needs of the one doing the criticizing rather something that you've done wrong. Maintain your emotional balance.

Basic Emotional Need #3: Personal Power

> God did not give us a spirit of timidity, but a spirit of power,
> of love and self-discipline (2 Timothy 1:7).

A sense of power is healthy and necessary when placed in perspective. It's needed to seek satisfaction of needs for safety and self-worth. Power is required to act on a vow. It's lacking in those who resign themselves to unmet needs.

Teenagers demonstrate belief in personal power. Often they feel invincible. The physical and emotional strength of youth empowers them to reach out and grab life by the tail. Discretion and measured use of power often escape them. Who hasn't known a teenager who drives too fast or loudly asserts his right to do the wrong thing? Adults with exaggerated expectations act this way. They overestimate abilities to achieve security and self-worth.

Toddlers provide an opposing example. They often behave as if they have no power at all. When tired, they insist they must be carried. When afraid, they demand to remain in the comfort of home. Adults who lack personal power give up in similar ways.

These behaviors are often accepted in children and teens. We make allowances for age and immaturity. These aren't the behaviors we expect from well-adjusted adults.

Power adjustment #1—lowering expectations. It's Friday afternoon. You left the office early to take Johnny to the doctor. You worked overtime all week to meet deadlines. Sally has soccer practice at five, and your husband expects dinner as usual. You have the power to make many people happy, but you aren't supermom. Superdads, superemployees, and superstudents all struggle with their own irrational expectations.

The sensation of power carries some people too far, leading to impulsive decisions and overcommitments. Friends become annoyed by broken promises. Co-workers take the blame for unfinished projects. Other people suffer when we overcommit and fail to deliver.

The enthusiasm of power may also hinder our intimacy with God. People with boundless power feel no need for God. This man can handle his problems without God. This woman doesn't have time to pray. This is not God's way. He wants to be our source of power because He has the power to complete His will in our lives.

Adjusting expectations in recovery from black moods often begins with cutting back on commitments. This means recognizing the limits to your power. Limiting hours of work or reducing obligations to church and school groups are some places to start. Give your vows a rest. Let go of your need to make the world safe. Release urges to prove your value to other people. Later, when your mood is rebalanced and your thinking is clear, will be a better time to carefully reengage your commitments. Early recovery should be a time of rest. Overcommitment will hinder your progress.

This need to set limits is clearly spelled out in a psychiatric hospital. When people are admitted to a psychiatric unit, they'e separated from responsibilities and reminded to limit expectations. Eating, sleeping, and talking about recovery are the limits of expected behavior. A woman who's overburdened with cares for her family is advised to let someone else worry about those problems for a while. A man obsessed with financial debts is told to forget about solving that problem for a few days. A time of separation from phone calls and e-mail helps them to recognize limits to their power and adjust expectations.

It's not necessary to check into a psychiatric hospital to adjust your commitments, but you will need help. Ask a friend or loved one to be your psychiatric nurse. Let her have the power for a while. She'll screen your phone calls and relieve you of responsibilities. A few days of rest will initiate a process of rebalancing moods.

Power adjustment #2—raising expectations. For people who resign themselves too easily, adjusting expectations means raising their beliefs in personal ability. Open your mind to God's opinion about your abilities. Seek a mentor or friend who can encourage your efforts to gain security or respect. Sometimes the help of a professional counselor is needed.

Realize that *your* God-given power will be different than mine. It will be different from that of your pastor or political leader. Satisfying your need for power will be found in fulfilling the dream God places in your heart. It will be standing up with courage to answer the desire He puts inside you. For some, it simply means regaining the confidence to go to the store. For others, it's starting a new job or relationship. This is something God wants for you and for me—to appreciate the power of His Spirit to influence the world through us.

Changing the way you think about your power will change the way you speak to other people at the store, the office, and family gatherings. This is the premise of cognitive therapy—changing the way you think will change the way you feel and behave. The goal of cognitive therapy is changing beliefs in order to reduce worries and relieve depression. The woman with a low sense of power will be asked to re-examine the evidence. Are the reasons you "can't" do that thing legitimate? Is the obstacle that big? Are you really that helpless?

In Christian counseling, a minister or elder may approach the same issues using God's Word. Can God provide satisfaction? Do life stories recorded in the Bible support this? Have you heard personal stories of people empowered by God? Again, the way out of dark moods is guided by clear thinking. Faith is believing and trusting in the power and goodwill of God despite the waves of emotion. Think deeply upon the power of God to create galaxies and brain cells. He can change your mood and your circumstances and lead you to people who can help. Think good thoughts and better feelings will follow. The apostle Paul, recognizing the power of positive thinking, said,

> Whatever is right, whatever is pure, whatever is lovely, whatever is admirable—if anything is excellent or praise-worthy—think about such things (Philippians 4:8).

The cognitive therapist and pastoral counselor can agree. If you focus on what you know to be true, dismissing fears of the past and future, you can develop the feeling of power to change the world around you. Change your thinking about power by pondering Scripture verses like this one:

> May the God of hope fill you with peace as you trust in him, so that you may overflow with hope by the power of the Holy Spirit (Romans 15:13).

Reach out. Touch faith. Give yourself permission to believe in your ability. Yesterday it may not have seemed possible. Today it is. God can use what we have. If we have only two fish and five loaves of bread, He can feed 5000 (see Luke 9:13-17). If we have willingness, with His gifts He can empower us to influence one life or 5000.

These changes in personality take time. As you adjust expectations about your power, continue to raise your expectations. Bodybuilders don't gain physical power in one workout. You won't develop emotional power in one afternoon. Engage one small challenge this month. Do it again sometime soon. Big accomplishments are built on a stack of smaller ones.

Keep your expectations in balance. There are many things you can't change, many things you can. Prayer, good counsel, and common sense will help you see the difference.

Expectation Tune-up

What beliefs about yourself need a tune-up? What memories need to be reprocessed? Are your beliefs about your safety, self-worth, or personal power out of balance?

Perhaps it's time to make some changes. Be willing to reconsider the events of your past and the impact you'll allow them to have on your life today. Allow yourself to look to the future with hopeful anticipation. Consider God's purpose for your life in the days that follow, and rest in the peace that He offers today. Find that new balance— one that makes peace with your past, looks with hope to the future, and rests in the goodness of God today.

Consider some professional help—a mental mechanic. Talking with another person may help you reconsider beliefs and expectations. Many counselors focus on your making peace with the past. Others concentrate on expectations about the future. The goal of both approaches is to find relief of dark moods in the present.

Much mental maintenance can be done on your own. As much as possible, surround yourself with emotionally balanced people. Healthy friendships can be like good counselors, reinforcing your feelings of safety, of goodness, and power to change the world. Get closer to God through small groups, praise music, and inspirational reading. It will help to change your self-image.

As healthy changes develop, keep the momentum going. Lasting change is built on repetition. Return to the practices that reinforce healthy expectations. To solidify healthy changes, you must repeat the steps that brought you this insight. Read this chapter again. Return to that section of the Bible that once lifted your spirit. Go back to the counselor who helped you to rise above feelings of inadequacy.

It is also important to recognize the limits of good parenting and counseling. Satisfying core needs depends on the healthy operation of brain cells. While childhood relationships have a major role in satisfying basic needs, brain-based temperaments also play a role. When a child is born with a tendency to overreact or underreact, satisfying core needs may be difficult. Criticism may have deeper and longer-lasting effects despite healthy parenting or good counsel. Medications can be used to reduce these sensitivities in childhood or later adult years. In clinical depression, the most effective treatments most often include both medication and counseling. Medications help to control the intensity of responses and keep challenges in perspective. They may facilitate the process of changing expectations in counseling.

Finally, adjust your expectations about what it means to recover from black moods. Recovery from depression does not eliminate sad days. Sad moods will come with loss and disappointment, but as you break free of depression, dark days won't appear as dark. Bright days will appear more often.

Action Items

- Satisfaction of the needs to feel safe and basically good about ourselves is necessary to maintain a healthy balance of mood. Envision one way to seek satisfaction of each basic need.

- Childhood vows are overreactions to basic (core) emotional needs. If you tend to overreact to unmet needs, think about how to release one self-imposed responsibility.

- Childhood resignations are signs of giving up too easily. If this is your tendency, then raise your expectation about one thing you can accomplish.

- Observe how your mood will improve as you stop overreacting or resigning too easily.

- Prayerfully list your needs and desires, and trust God to rightly adjust your expectations.

- Look for a new balance between gratitude for the way you are and the faith to make changes.

Chapter 16

Revise Relationships with Others

"In everything, do to others what you would have them do to you."

JESUS, IN MATTHEW 7:12

When I was a psychiatrist with the army's 82nd Airborne Division, I met a young lieutenant who was depressed, consumed with anger about his wife's affair. The "emotional tumor" was big. It altered his ability to manage his unit and was destroying his good health. He developed asthma, high blood pressure, and stomach ulcers. Medications from numerous doctors didn't seem to be working. He was referred for psychiatric help.

He refused to discuss his wife's affair or her apology. He became obsessed with a quest to discover imagined new encounters. He chased an uninvolved man down the freeway with a shotgun at his side. Black moods began to dominate his mind. He lost his job, his marriage, and his health rather than consider a process of forgiveness. He expected others to forgive, but he couldn't do the same.

Granting forgiveness isn't natural. The more natural response to being hurt is to fight back, to make the other person pay. Two people get hurt in these angry acts of retribution. Forgiveness, on the other hand, is a carefully considered response that helps to heal the relationship. Forgiveness is a gift that benefits both sides of the relationship. It releases the other person from payment due. It also removes a tumor of bitterness from the one holding resentment. Holding on to bitterness alters our personalities and moods and interferes with the development of new, healthy relationships. Extracting the tumor of bitterness makes conflicted relationships less toxic and allows new ones to flourish.

Healthy forgiveness is not the act of a powerless individual. In healthy relationships, granting forgiveness is paired with the expectation of mutual respect. Healthy forgiveness both releases the offender from past debt and changes our expectations of the relationship. You might forgive an angry dog for biting your hand, but the reasonable person makes changes in his or her relationship with that dog. On the other hand, *accepting* a pattern of offense in relationships isn't a sign of healthy forgiveness.

Adding a requirement for respect, after the offense, is a process of setting up boundaries. It means developing and stating expectations of how you believe you should be treated. It includes consequences for honoring or dishonoring your requests. Boundary expectations are not commandments written in stone, but a flexible set of rules for living with and loving other people. They should be changed as we mature and develop better understanding.

"Do unto others as you would have them do unto you," and expect honorable responses in return. In relationally healthy people, others will respect your boundaries as you respect theirs. Clearly, this does not always happen. Still, carefully making expectations known is your half of a healthy relationship—the responses of other people are out of your hands. Do what is right, come what may.

A new emotional language

Revising relationships is like learning a new language, a process of changing the way you speak to other people. As you revamp relationships, you'll learn to set up new boundaries and forgive more readily. You'll learn to say no at times you have previously said yes. You'll find new ways to forgive, letting go of destructive resentments.

If you grew up speaking Spanish, that's probably the way you prefer to talk with other people. But speaking Spanish in an English-speaking situation will lead to miscommunication. In a similar way, unclear relationship boundaries lead to misunderstandings and strife.

We all have a tendency to fall back into old ways of dealing with stress in a crisis. As a bilingual man may drift back into his native language when feeling overwhelmed, we all tend to revert to old ways under stress. Your challenging times of today provide opportunities to relearn some behaviors under stress that will stick with you in the future. If you can maintain good boundaries and respond with forgiveness under stress, you'll find it much easier in days ahead—a new second language will begin to emerge.

Adult–Child Roles in Relationships

Maturity is not simply a process of getting old. Some adults act like children, and some offspring act like parents. Assuming the adult role in relationships is a practice of reasoned self-sacrifice, not merely the result of passing years.

Parents have the responsibility of setting limits for children and maintaining emotional balance when disagreements arise. In relationships with other adults, we have similar roles—requesting that others respect our positions, and managing our moods at points of disagreement. When relationships proceed in this way, good things happen. However, when one adult acts like a child, the other must take the role of parent. When both act like children, bad outcomes are inevitable.

Children want what they want right now. It takes time and training for them to learn a healthy balance of give and take in relationships. Young children tend to react with strong emotion when things don't go their way. Parents have the job of containing that emotion. When a child makes bad choices and reacts with foolish anger, the role of the parent is to keep one eye on right behavior and one on right emotion.

Mature adults have learned how to contain emotion without being pulled into destructive conflicts.

Just as a cup contains bubbling soda water without becoming part of the beverage, a mature parent contains the feelings of an angry child without becoming part of that emotion. The parent recognizes that the child is overreacting, and she keeps her emotional balance. She contains the passion by listening but not overreacting herself. She responds in a calm state of mind, imposing reasonable consequences for words and behaviors.

A similar scenario may occur with adults. In childish fits of emotion, people say and do things that hurt. The mature response at this point is to contain the emotion, being mindful of what we believe to be right, and to respond respectfully from that position. The guy at the office, the lady at the store, and the adolescent sitting in the row ahead of you at church will each act a bit like children at times. You'll be challenged to contain destructive emotions, request reasonable respect, and forgive in a thoughtful way. As you take these steps, levels of stress will subside, brain cells will be spared, and your moods will become lighter.

The Process of Granting Forgiveness

> Everyone says that forgiveness is a lovely idea, until they have something to forgive. —C.S. Lewis, *Mere Christianity*

Forgiveness rarely happens with the simple words "I forgive you." The deeper the offense, the larger the tumor of resentment. The bigger the emotional tumor, the more injurious it is to self-esteem and relationships. When resentments about past wrongs are allowed to remain in our hearts, they seep into our present-day relations, creating bitterness and dark moods. Friends will notice that something is wrong and wonder why we seem so unhappy. Sometimes we aren't aware of the connections ourselves.

The process of forgiveness outlined in this section is organized in steps. As a guy who likes order and labels for things, I've summarized the changes I see operating in people who let go of resentment. This is a process for letting go of bad feelings and revising relationships, not a rigid prescription.

> ## Seven Steps of Forgiveness
>
> 1. List offenses
> 2. Express discontent
> 3. Consider confrontation
> 4. Listen to reply
> 5. Consider your role
> 6. Cancel the debt 70 x 7
> 7. Set up new boundaries

1. List offenses. If you want to forgive an offense, you must know what it is. This may seem obvious, but it's often overlooked. The more clearly you see the wrong that was done and the feelings it created, the better able you'll be to manage your response. Forgiveness starts with collecting facts and recalling feelings.

Remember the point of greatest hurt. Is there some point in time, some location in your home, where the bad thing most noticeably occurred? Even if the offense was repeated many times, try to focus on one moment that stands out. That's the point to begin.

What are the facts? Was it morning or evening? Where were you? Where was the other person? What was going on in the room? What was said? What was done?

How did you feel at the moment of the offense? What were the feelings that followed? Were you angry, sad, or embarrassed? Remember these facts and feelings. Be ready to share them with somebody else.

2. Express discontent. "Expressing discontent" is a nice way of saying, "State what makes you angry." It's a clinical-sounding phrase that emphasizes you're doing something deliberate, not simply rambling on about vague feelings. Expressing discontent is explaining what is bothering you in a way that doesn't incite anger and payback from the other person.

For the believer, a good place to begin expressing discontent is in prayer with God. Find a quiet place, free of distraction, and open up to Him. King David was good at this. The psalms are sprinkled with his tears and expressions of frustration.

Expressing discontent is vital to healthy relationships, especially when you're moving toward forgiveness. Verbalizing feelings makes them easier to manage. Emotions seem less powerful when put into words and shared with someone else. This is a major benefit of counseling—having someone to listen to the feeling-words that come out of your mouth. That simple exchange is somehow remarkably relieving. Close friendships share this characteristic by providing a safe place to be open with feelings.

Stanley, one of my patients, is quite skilled at expressing emotion with his family. When dark moods well up, he finds a quiet place to talk with his wife. This often results in tears as he pours out words of regret. After several minutes, he feels purged. These moments of emotional release help him release unhealthy feelings that might otherwise pull him back into depression.

He has expressed himself in this way many times over the past three years, and it has allowed him to reduce his dose of antidepressant. The usual dose of his medication is 100 to 150 milligrams. Stanley is now able to keep black moods away with 25 milligrams of medication and a pile of handkerchiefs.

3. Consider confrontation. Sometimes, expression of discontent should be done with the one who offended you. Talk to someone else first. Weigh the risks and benefits of having such a conversation. Consider the other person's possible responses and how you'll end the conversation. The offender may answer your expressions with denial and more conflict.

When confronted with past wrongs, many people will deny the

event ever happened or deny the impact of their actions. The value of expressing your discontent is not simply to solicit an apology or empathy. You will benefit from growing in self-assertiveness and making peace with your past.

Expressing your discontent in measured, considered words will help you validate, in your own mind, that the injustice was wrong, and that the other person's disregard of your feelings wasn't acceptable then—nor is it acceptable now. People who fail to develop this realization risk repeated offense. Those who learn to speak up against offense are less likely to be offended in that way again.

Discussing the event will also cause the other person to pause and consider her behavior before doing it again. Confronting the offender benefits others in this way. She learns that someone will hold her accountable for bad decisions.

Express your discontent with tact and moderation. The goal of confrontation is building healthier relationships, not destroying the other person. Recognize that confrontation may lead to angry self-defense. This is less likely to happen with measured expression of your own anger. Be ready to contain the emotional response of the other person and take the next right steps. (This will look like the behavior of a reasonable parent helping her child contain distressing feelings.)

Sometimes it isn't possible or prudent to confront an offender. He may be dangerous or dead. She may have moved far away. It may be more appropriate to write a letter describing the facts and feelings, even if you never mail the letter. Still, it's important to develop an attitude that confrontation is an option. Maintain the belief that you will protest similar offenses in the future.

The empty chair. Talking about deep emotional injuries is hard. It seems easier to let past problems remain past problems, keeping them bottled up in forgotten corners of your memory. Sometimes that *is* better. However, when these memories leak out and cause problems in present-day relationships, it may be better to let them out and discuss them.

One way to get these emotions out is to talk about them in

counseling. Some therapists use a process termed the *empty-chair tech-nique*. In this method of emotional release the client is asked to speak to an empty chair as if the offending party were sitting in that chair. I have found this technique quite helpful.

Rachael, a middle-aged woman who had been verbally degraded by her mother throughout her childhood, could hardly mention the abuse due to fear and guilt instilled by her early life experiences. She came for help with anxiety and depression that kept her paralyzed, fearful of leaving her home or defending herself when challenged.

First we talked about a series of abusive events that happened during her elementary-to-high-school years. Then I asked her to speak to an empty chair as if her mother were sitting there. She wouldn't have been able to say anything about the abuse directly to her mother. It felt awkward and scary for her to consider talking to the chair. Past complaints to her mother had been followed by punishment. After a few of our meetings together, she was ready.

She told her mother—the chair—how she truly felt. She proceeded to talk about specific memories. Cursing and harsh tones came out of this otherwise timid and mild-mannered young woman. Her face got red and her pulse quickened. Her neck became beet-red. For the first time in her life, she was able to stand up for herself and speak against a pattern of abuse.

The exercise made her very uneasy. After expressing discontent she told me, "I hate that chair." During the next several weeks of counsel-ing, she watched the empty chair out of the corner of her eye—angry about the way she had been hurt and guarding herself against a feared response.

It helped. Rachael became more open with her true feelings. She began to feel a greater level of comfort standing up to the abuse of her mother and others. Following this catharsis of anger and hurt, she grew in her ability to forgive. In later sessions, she wanted to talk about why her mother had treated her so harshly. She recognized the chain of abuse that had started with her grandmother (in reality, probably generations before that). Her mother had been treated in a similar way. Rachael was breaking the chain. She still falls back into feelings of helpless anger, but she climbs out of the hopelessness more quickly. She speaks her mind, listens to the reply with less trepidation, and forgives more easily.

4. Listen to the reply. In listening to someone's response to your expression of discontent, it may become apparent that the offender has been hurt by someone else. Many abusive parents learned their behaviors from their own parents. They carry around resentments that are displaced onto other people.

Understanding this dynamic does not excuse bad behavior, but it provides an opportunity for seeing your role in a new light. Unfair treatment by other people often has more to do with old issues in the mind of that person than our own present-day behavior. Placing those hurts in the context of the woundedness of an offender may help. You won't be able to erase the painful memories that cause disrespect by the other person, but you can reduce further strain in the relationship by recognizing this pattern. Recognizing the source of unfair treatment will help you hold on to the notion that "I am a pretty good person, despite disrespect from others." It will reduce your stress levels and risk for black moods.

5. Consider your part. As you listen to the other person's response, keep an open mind about your own contribution to the problem. As you express discontent, be willing to listen. Modeling respect and willingness to change can be part of the process.

Consider your own role in the conflict. Maybe you did something to provoke the offense. Maybe the offense was not really that bad. Your perception of events may be biased by your own tempest of emotion. Depression has a way of clouding clear thinking. More commonly, however, those in black moods focus on their own shortcomings, dismissing the role of others in conflict.

6. Cancel the debt 70 x 7. When a businessman releases a bad debt, he may do so partly out of sympathy, but he also does it because it makes sense. Collecting the debt may cause more aggravation than the debt itself. Forgiving a personal offense also makes practical sense. It may feel as if you are giving up some right to retribution but, in the end, you reap the profits of liberation from bitterness.

Releasing resentment brings freedom to new relationships you form—baggage from the past is dropped. Holding on to resentments, on the other hand, increases the likelihood of your repeating the same type of relationship in the future. A woman abused in one marriage may leave the man and marry another abuser if she fails to forgive the first. If she holds on to bitterness about mistreatment, it will interfere with her relationships with men in the future. She will become so focused on the dysfunctional type of relationship that she may inadvertently look for it and recreate it. Releasing negative emotions through expression and forgiveness helps restore emotional freedom.

New Testament accounts of Jesus Christ's behavior provide great examples of healthy boundaries and forgiveness. When disrespected in the temple, He chased out the money traders (see Matthew 21:12). When struck by Roman guards, He demanded they justify their behavior or stop (see John 18:23). When crucified for our sins, He asked God to forgive us (see Luke 23:34). There is a time to confront disrespect and a time to release our right to retribution.

Christ counsels us to forgive our neighbor "seventy times seven" times (Matthew 18:22). That's a lot of forgiving. This verse may refer to forgiving the same event over and over. It may also relate to forgiving the same person for repeated offenses.

If the incident you're forgiving created deep hurt and resentment, you may need to release it many times in your mind. Deeply held feelings have a way of creeping back into our hearts. The first act of forgiveness may release the bulk of resentment, but little seeds may remain and sprout up in moments of high stress. In periods of our life like these, we must release our right to retribution again—70 x 7 times.

We may also need to forgive the same person again and again. This doesn't mean ignoring the event or helplessly exposing ourselves to further mistreatment. Common sense tells us to change our behavior, to get out of the way of dangerous people. A mature Christian response can be to express discontent, confront bad behavior, and set up new boundaries—number 7 in the process of forgiveness.

Establish New Boundaries

> Boundaries are a "litmus test" for the quality of our relation-ships. —Henry Cloud and John Townsend, *Boundaries*

In personal relationships, boundaries are limitations we set on the behavior of other people, borders that keep people where they belong. When boundaries break down, conflict and stress increase, along with the likelihood of dark moods. Many hurt feelings can be avoided by having clearly stated boundaries. When I respect your boundaries and you respect mine, we get along quite well.

Setting limits. Many people come for counseling when the demands of other people become overwhelming. Healing moments come as they recognize the limits to their power and the need to place limits on others.

Sometimes, setting boundaries is a negotiating process. For an office assistant, it may mean telling her boss that she can work late tonight but cannot take on a new project. For a mother with small children, it may mean reading them a story and taking them to the playground, but refusing to go to the store. It means saying, "I can do A and B, but I cannot do C."

Substitute the things you *can* do for A and B, and the thing you *can't* do for C. There are limits to the things we can do for other people. Setting up boundaries in this way helps them understand that we respect their needs but are mindful of our own limitations. It is a step in revising relationships and healing black moods.

Don't do that. Sometimes setting up boundaries is as simple as saying no. For Rob, it began with his sister and extended to the rest of his family. He was a single father who maintained close ties with extended family. He lived in a small apartment and was visited quite often by his sister, Betty. They shared concerns about work and family and supported each other.

Betty's visits, however, became disturbing when she went to the bathroom. On most of her visits, she would howl in pain as she completed her bathroom activities. This was a common occurrence, and it had gone on for so long that Rob had lost appreciation for how grossly disrespectful it was to others in the apartment building.

Permitting the display and enduring the distress it created was a sign of Rob's failure to set up good boundaries. He knew he felt tense when his sister announced plans to drop by, but he couldn't explain his uneasiness. The problem became clear as he talked about his family in counseling. Betty had a habit of dumping her bad feelings on Rob. Moments in the bathroom were just one example. He recounted numerous unreasonable demands and displays of emotion. The offensiveness of her behavior was easy to acknowledge once he stopped to consider it.

Stopping the bathroom drama was the first step. The second and third steps included setting limits on the behavior of his children and co-workers. He learned it was okay to say no. He learned that his family and co-workers wouldn't spurn him if he insisted on respectful behavior. The freedom that grew within new healthy boundaries helped lift him out of dark moods.

Not my problem. From our early years on the playground, we learn that it's easier to blame someone else than take punishment for wrong behavior. This tendency doesn't disappear after childhood, but adults are more skilled at passing the blame. When we feel bad about our thought life or behavior, we often put those bad feelings on somebody else. Somewhere, sometime, you will be blamed for something that wasn't your fault.

If I feel guilty about not spending enough time with the kids, I may suggest to my wife that she's not being a good mother. If she feels guilty about spending too much money, she may criticize me about my purchase of a new pair of shoes. Psychologists call this *projection*—projecting your bad feelings onto another person. He's the bad one. She's the disrespectful one. It's an unhealthy way to deal with the feelings that disturb us, but it seems easier than dealing with the issues in ourselves.

In disagreements and arguments, we will do well to watch out for this dynamic. When someone tells you that you're irresponsible or bad, it may be true. On the other hand, it's also quite possible that someone is projecting his own sense of irresponsibility on you. If you accept the false blame, then he's succeeded in making his problem your problem. You feel bad about yourself because you've identified with his projection. The psychological term for this successful passage of blame is *projective identification*. You have identified with the false projection and made it part of your identity.

Maintaining good boundaries means keeping other people's stuff out of *your* stuff. When conflicts arise and you're criticized for something that doesn't feel right, take some time to consider the possibility of projective identification. The bad thing being spoken of may not be your problem. The responsibility for the problem and the stress that comes with it may be dismissed in this way.

If the problem isn't yours, it's not your responsibility to fix it. Even so, you may try to help. Sometimes, you may be able to help the other person reconcile the bad feelings he's projected onto you. Careful reassurance and redirection may help him resolve the bad feelings without projecting them.

This is mine. A fence around a yard sends a message: "This is my space." Walls and doorways of a house send another message: "Don't come in here without asking permission." Even these clear boundaries can be challenged.

A 50-year-old woman bought a three-level townhouse. She and her husband had plans to make it a nice place to retire. Rosalie was kindhearted, so when her mother asked to move in, she consented. Rosalie had learned to honor her mother, but her mother had learned to take advantage of her. From her early years, Rosalie had learned she couldn't set limits on her mother.

When move-in day arrived, Rosalie's mother demanded that her daughter and her husband move into the basement. Mother would take over the upper two floors. When Rosalie came up to the kitchen, her mother ordered her back into the basement. This became the way things would go in the new home.

When Rosalie challenged this arrangement, her mother called her selfish. She identified with that projection; feeling selfish and ashamed, she retreated to the basement again.

In helping her to break through her black moods, she and I talked about boundaries. She felt powerless to erect them. She felt conflicted by opposing feelings. One feeling told her to honor her mother (see Exodus 20:12). Another one told her it was wrong for parents to take advantage of their children (see 2 Corinthians 12:14). Many months of counseling and conversations with friends could not convince her to take control of her townhouse.

Rather than engage in further conflict, she sold the townhouse and found a retirement village for her mother. Her black moods resolved themselves—she began to smile and speak in lighthearted tones again. She joked and laughed. She packed up her belongings and her husband and moved to the other side of the country. Only from 2000 miles away could she say, "This is mine, and you can't have it."

The virtue of taking charge of what is yours should be balanced with generosity. Biblical teachings illustrate the value of both. One passage speaks of a man who failed to wisely invest the money given him to take care of. His smaller amount was taken from him and given to another man who had a larger amount (Matthew 25:28). An example of protecting possessions is the story of virgins who refused to give away their oil (Matthew 25:9). On the other hand, the life of Christ provides examples of giving up what we have to help others. Christ gave up all of His earthly possessions for us. Clearly, protecting what is ours must be balanced with freely chosen sacrifice for others. It is part of the healthy adult role.

Managing possessions is also a matter of *stewardship.* Christian financial consultant Ray Linder describes stewardship as a responsibility to manage God's resources. He describes the tension that many people feel as they are pulled between beliefs that godly people are poor (money is evil) and that godly people are prosperous (money is a reward from God).[1] In *Boundaries,* Cloud and Townsend note,

> Being created in God's image also means ownership, or stewardship. As Adam and Eve were given dominion over the earth to subdue it and rule it, we are also given stewardship over our time, energy, talents, values, feelings, behavior, money.[2]

The authors draw a careful distinction between stewardship and selfishness. It is important to take ownership of the blessings entrusted to us, while not neglecting our responsibility to love other people. In healthy relationships, we neither focus too long on our own desires nor allow others to trample over us with theirs. As stewards of God's gifts, we have a responsibility to protect, invest, and distribute our resources. These are signs of good stewardship and healthy stress management.

Growing Relationships

As black moods creep in, friends and family are pushed to the side— sometimes by irritability, sometimes by social retreat. Acquaintances go first. Friendships and family members go next. The network of social connections breaks apart as people slide into illness. Part of recovery from depression includes re-establishing those bonds with other people.

As doctors prepare patients for discharge from the hospital, they look for people in the community to help support their recovery. Doctors and nurses realize that prevention of relapse into more serious depression depends upon the help of others.

The development of black moods and the loss of connections takes weeks or months to occur. Likewise, it will take time and effort to reestablish connections. Reconnecting with friends and loved ones takes effort. It involves forgiveness, new boundaries, and rekindling affections.

In *The Five Love Languages,* author Gary Chapman suggests five concrete ways to develop stronger ties with our spouses. Single or married, the suggestions apply to our wider social connections as well. These five ways of expressing love are 1) words of affirmation, 2) quality time, 3) giving gifts, 4) acts of service, and 5) physical touch:[3]

1. *Learn what the other person needs to hear.* Some need to be forgiven and assured that things are okay. In the context of core needs, those with strong needs for self-worth will need praise for the good things they've done. Such affirmations will help to heal the injuries caused by harsh criticisms of the past.

2. *Some need quality time with the loved one.* Learn to listen and laugh again with friends. Pick one night of the week and call it date night with your spouse. Enjoy some face-to-face time with other people.

3. *Give a gift.* Depression is a very self-centered state of mind. Giving gifts is a practical way to get your attention off your problems and onto somebody else. Gifts are symbols of personal sacrifice and focus on another person's desires.

4. *What act of service does your friend or loved one most appreciate?* Take someone to breakfast. Wash someone's car. Prayer can be an act of serving. Asking God to help someone is an act of spiritual service. These are tangible signs that you're emerging from black moods and appreciating the value of your contributions to the world.

5. *Touch somebody.* Shake someone's hand. Physical touch establishes a closer connection. Give someone else a hug or pat on the back. Spend an intimate evening with your spouse. In the midst of dark moods, interest in sex often disappears. With renewal of mood comes growing intimacy in the marriage relationship.

Each of these expressions of love is easily appreciated, but each person has a preference for one over another. Understanding their inclination depends on your appreciating, through empathy, how that person feels.

Empathy

Empathy is the capacity to participate in another person's feelings. In communication, empathy has two parts. One part is listening to the words coming out of the other person's mouth. The other part is listening to unspoken feelings.

Empathy is a process of listening to emotions and feeling the same way. Scientists suggest that people who empathize well with others experience similar brain changes.[4] The brain regions active in the one talking about her sadness are also active in the one doing the listening. Neuroscientists call this phenomenon *mirroring* of brain-cell activity. As you listen and feel the way another person feels, your brain will mirror the chemical activity. This is the level of emotional connectivity that builds strong social ties.

In the book *Soul Talk,* Larry Crabb encourages us to ask, "What's going on in this person's soul?" He suggests a process of conversation that allows the psychological and spiritual needs of the other person to come forth and then discusses these needs in a healing manner. He encourages the use of silence—a time to be quiet and listen—"allowing the powerful life of Christ to surface within us and be released in the words we speak."[5]

The Golden Rule calls us to do unto others as we would have them do unto us—love other people as you would like to be loved. Imagine what a new, caring relationship might look like for you. As you spend time in the new relationship, practice exercising empathy. While depression leads to loneliness, recovery enables intimacy.

Finally, consider your role as a "wounded healer." Recognize the hurt in someone else, and ask God to help and comfort that person through you. As one who has overcome black moods, your words have special meaning to someone still stuck in that place. Your story—that life can be good—will have more power than any book because you have lived through the darkness.

Action Items

- Resentments become tumors of bitterness that choke out new relationships. Begin letting them go.
- Express discontent.
- Listen to the other person's point and consider your contribution to the problem.
- You may need to forgive one person 70 x 7 times for repeated offenses, or you may need to forgive the same offense 70 x 7 times in your mind.
- Remember this: Forgiveness + New Boundaries = Healthy Relationships.
- Build some reasonable new boundaries. You can help other people by doing A and B, but not C.
- Empathy is a process of listening to the words and feelings of the one speaking to you. Learn to listen to feelings.

Chapter 17

Track with the Holy Spirit

"When he, the Spirit of truth, comes, he will guide you into all truth."

JESUS, IN JOHN 16:13

The Holy Spirit is God—His presence among us. Jesus spoke of the Holy Spirit as the Helper, that Person of the Trinity we may experience in day-to-day life: "The Helper, the Holy Spirit, whom the Father will send in My name, He will teach you all things" (John 4:26 NKJV).

How the Helper teaches us things, changes brain-cell function, or heals any illness is a mystery. This type of healing isn't natural—that is, originating with chemical change or counseling insight. Spiritual healing is a *super*natural experience of God's touch, an outcome of a personal relationship that defies our description. There is no dosage to calculate or psychotherapy technique to evaluate, only one childlike choice to make—to trust, to move forward in faith. All we need do is have humility, ask God to show Himself, and wait for His help and guidance.

This chapter describes ways to open the door to your soul. As you pray and wait for God to respond, the Helper will guide and shape you in the process of renewal He has in mind for you. The "T" of SMART Steps stands for "Tracking with the Spirit." As Paul said, "Since we live by the Spirit, let us keep in step with the Spirit" (Galatians 5:25).

This is both the place to begin and the place to end, both the pinnacle of recovery and an integral part of each earlier step.

Acknowledge Your Powerlessness

Spiritual renewal begins on your knees. On your knees you look weak. On your knees you *are* weak, but your weakness can be made strong. This is where the Holy Spirit will meet you—at the end of your own resources and abilities.

Begin your steps toward renewal by giving up control—surrender your weaknesses and wishes to God. Along with the apostle Paul, believe what God says: "My power is made perfect in weakness" (2 Corinthians 12:9). God expresses His strength through broken, helpless people—those who recognize Who has the power and who doesn't.

The Spirit of God is waiting beside you, passionately wanting to transform your helplessness into new life. We live in God's world, and He is in charge. Whether you find yourself in a crowded bus station or moment of solitary sadness, the Spirit is prepared to comfort and help you like Jesus. Adversity and illness are signals to meet with the Helper, not meaningless distractions in your day.

Surrender can be the first step to overcoming your difficulty. At that point of readiness, may you catch a glimpse of God's wonderful generosity. Like a bolt of lightning illuminates the midnight sky, your spirit can be filled with the light of His presence, and your pathway to recovery can become clear.

Reset Priorities

Powerlessness is a perfect point to allow God to reset your agendas as you relinquish your own priorities and let Him be in charge. One way to get started is to make a written list of your worries. Name the things that hurt you and the fears that keep you awake at night. Naming the worries begins a process of catharsis—getting the bad stuff out of your mind and onto a piece of paper. Move your most important worries to the top and the least important ones to the bottom. This emotional to-do list will help you to decide where to focus your energy.

Now change that inventory of worries into a list of items to hand over to God. Think deeply about this list and pray about each item. Tell your New Boss how you honestly feel about each item on the list and ask for His answers—His wisdom. *What am I to learn? What am I to do?*

> If any of you lacks wisdom, he should ask God, who gives generously to all without finding fault, and it will be given to him (James 1:5).

Wisdom often gets lost in depression, as daily worries and hurts get jumbled together into a difficult-to-manage emotional mess. Grief and fear become tangled up with self-criticism and hopelessness. Handing over your worries to God and allowing Him to determine the outcome will put them in the hands of someone with the power and wisdom to guide you to real answers.

Give Your Worries to God

Worry is a gateway type of wrong, leading to self-doubt and God-doubt. A little worry seems harmless, even necessary and helpful. Chronic worry, however, leads to stress-hormone responses that, as we've seen, can damage brain cells and lead to dark moods. Worry is fuel for depression.

Faith—trust—extinguishes worry. Believing that God cares for you and knows what He's doing snuffs out little worries that might otherwise grow to consume you. "Faith" is more than some vague notion that God will take care of you. Faith means we trust our relationship with Him, not in the outcome, honoring Him regardless of outcomes.

Your faith will be sharpened as you clarify the ways in which you trust the Problem Solver. Boldly consider the best and worst outcomes for each problem on your list. Be open and honest about your greatest hopes and worst fears, creating an inventory of possibilities like the one in the chart below. Then expect the Helper to transform your list of worries into a record of the ways you are relying on Him. Faith is trusting the Wise One during the best or worst circumstances your mind might imagine.

Like Abraham, who remained focused during the worst moments a father could imagine, keep your eyes on the Author of life, not the events of today. Abraham laid his son on an altar of sacrifice with the full realization that the All-Powerful One had the authority to spare his child's life or not (see Genesis 22:9). Abraham focused on the Father, not on worries, and God took care of Abraham.

Sample Worry List			
Worry	*No Change*	*Worst Case*	*Best Case*
Spouse is angry	Resentment	Divorce	Intimacy
Child is sick	Sickness	Death	Healing
Your worry			

Live in Trust

In our best thinking, we know that the Creator of the universe must know what He's doing. Trusting the Designer of galaxies and brain cells seems like no leap of faith, but moving that belief from a logical place in our minds to an emotional place in our hearts is not easy, especially in depression. Hardships have a way of chipping away our trust that the Creator will listen to our prayers, care about our needs, and keep us full of peace.

When we get stuck on past hurts and our fears about tomorrow, trust gives way to worry. It's not easy for a husband who is estranged from his wife to hold on to trust regardless of end results. Harder still for the mother of a critically ill child to pray for healing and accept that a cure may not come. Can you pray for the best but accept the worst, if that is God's answer?

This kind of trust grows out of a maturing relationship. Each spiritual step you take toward God is met by a thousand from Him. As you take one step of trust, the Holy Spirit will empower you to take another. This is the miracle of tracking with the Spirit, of learning to take one more step of trust.

Staying on this track means continuing to entrust each new challenge to God. Just as athletic excellence requires persistent commitment, the development of spiritual vitality depends on day-by-day exercise. Victorious athletes focus on the basics, not fad videos or newfangled equipment. In a similar way, maturing Christians pay attention to the basics—prayer, meditation, and biblical guidance—choosing to respond to life challenges with these disciplines.

My meditation of choice focuses on the words from an old hymn, "Living by Faith." I like the way the song leads me to surrender my desires and fears about tomorrows. The way of thinking that underlies the words helps me to hand over my worries to God. Some of my patients find help in this meditation as well. One woman who was in the midst of divorce used the meditation to keep her head from exploding when her husband refused to share custody of the children. She has learned and relearned to trust God regardless of possibilities.

Take a moment to think about the message of this song and how it applies to your worries.

> I care not today what tomorrow may bring,
> If *shadow* or *sunshine* or *rain*.
> The Lord I know ruleth over everything,
> And all of my worry is vain.[1]

God controls the shadows, the sunshine, and the rain in your life. He can change each raindrop, teardrop, or moment of hardship. Your worry is useless—vain.

To deepen your trust, return to your list of worries. Blend the best and worst outcomes with the trust expressed in the song. Substitute the words "no change" for "shadow." Insert your best-case and worst-case outcomes for the words "sunshine" and "rain." If you don't know the melody of the song, consider it a poem.

For a husband worried about his wife's plan to leave, the poem might become...

> I care not today what tomorrow may bring,
> If *no change,* or *reunion, or divorce.*
> The Lord I know ruleth over everything,
> And all of my worry is vain.

For the mother worried about her child's serious illness, the poem becomes...

> I care not today what tomorrow may bring,
> If *no change,* or *healing,* or *death.*
> The Lord I know ruleth over everything,
> And all of my worry is vain.

For each of the worries on your list, the poem becomes...

> I care not today what tomorrow may bring,
> If *no change,* or _____, or _____.
> The Lord I know ruleth over everything,
> And all of my worry is vain.

Consider meeting each day with an outlook like this. Tomorrow will bring new worries, and old worries may circle back again. When these challenges to your belief and trust become gnawing distractions, make a list of the worries and give it away. Your empty spiritual efforts will end as you give your control to the Controller.

Talk with *The* Counselor

> I will ask the Father, and he will give you another Counselor (John 14:16).

The Holy Spirit listens better than any human counselor. As Christ prepared for physical death, He told His disciples that He would send a helper, a spiritual counselor to continue His loving involvement in their lives. Unburden yourself of your feelings in prayer, and the Counselor will listen to your deepest hurt and give direction to your mind.

Relying on the Counselor to do this is sometimes hard. Christians in the middle of depression usually have trouble with prayer. Brain-cell imbalances make it hard to maintain concentration and hold on to hope. Ironically, when people most need the reassurance and sense of purpose that comes from prayer, depression can make the words feel like a waste of breath.

Don't stop praying! If you feel alone and alienated, tell God. If you feel angry and abandoned, say so! Like David, who cried out in angry sadness, be open and honest with God. David shouted, "Break the teeth in their mouths, O God...like a stillborn child, may they not see the sun" (Psalm 58:6-9). Rather than let anger and sadness separate him from God, David used prayer as an avenue of expressing his heartache.

Expressive—Submissive Prayer

- Tell God how you feel
- Ask for your desire
- Surrender to His will

Prayer is also about God's intervention and healing. The prophet Jeremiah believed this. "I will restore you to health and heal your wounds," he wrote (Jeremiah 30:17). Most Americans agree that prayer promotes healing, including that of black moods. A survey of religious practices made by *U.S. News and World Report* found that when people pray about their health, 65 percent pray for restoration of mental health.[2]

Open up to God and ask for what you need. Sometimes the Physician heals the body; sometimes He heals the mind. Whatever His answer, which will be according to His insight, the Counselor has a peace plan for you. As Paul told the Philippians,

> Do not be anxious about anything, but in everything, by prayer and petition, with thanksgiving, present your requests to God. And the peace of God, which transcends all understanding, will guard your hearts and your minds in Christ Jesus (Philippians 4:6-7).

Prayer has less to do with the Counselor finding solutions to your problems than with getting your relationship right with Him. Prayer is not about convincing God to execute your will. It's about spiritual connection, a relationship between spirits—your spirit and His spirit— a process of becoming one in purpose with the Counselor.

··

His way, not yours
··

In the midst of a frustrating relationship with his girlfriend, an angry executive told me that he was in "silent protest" against God. "Prayer doesn't change the course of events," he said. "So why should I pray? He's not going to answer my prayers." This otherwise intelligent Christian forgot how prayer works. Rather than asking for guidance from the Counselor, he wanted the Counselor to see things *his* way.

Jesus' model of prayer—the "Lord's Prayer"—has little to say about getting God to see things our way. It has much more to say about getting our minds in line with His will. The Lord's Prayer starts with respect for God the Father's position and submission to His will, and includes a brief request for physical needs—"Give us today our daily bread." It ends with an appeal for forgiveness and a request for help to do things His way (see Matthew 6:9-13).

Think Deeply upon Simple Truth

A muscular young man who was a patient of mine told me that depression made it hard for him to pick up a Bible. He clearly had enough physical strength. It was the mental perseverance he lacked. So we talked about simplifying his Bible study by focusing on bite-sized portions of Scripture. Thinking over short verses made it easier for him to let God's Word percolate through his mind.

Another client, a church-history student, focused on the Hebrew name for God—*Yahweh*. He claimed that this was the easiest way to think deeply upon the majesty of God. "It's so effortless that you can speak Yahweh's name without moving your lips," he explained. You can try it also. Get alone. Close your eyes and focus on the name of Yahweh. Breathe slowly and deeply. With each slow breath in, make the sound *yah*. With each slow breath out, make the sound *weh*. Repeat the exercise again and again, considering the presence of God. When complicated feelings clog up your thinking, this short meditation may help clear the fog.

A 60-year-old grandmother uses the twenty-third psalm ("The Lord is my shepherd..."), along with medication, to prevent dark moods— a combined prescription for her habit of worry at bedtime. In quiet, she slowly considers the meaning of each phrase and how the words fit her life for that day. Excessive worry, the fuel for depression, is extinguished as she recalls that the Shepherd takes care of her needs and those of her children.

Connect to a Spiritual Network

Spiritual renewal is speeded up by connections with spiritually healthy people. If you want renewed hope, surround yourself with hopeful people. If you want renewed joy, get together with people who enjoy their relationship with God. In any domain of your life, surround yourself with people you want to be like. Healthy spirituality rubs off from spiritually healthy people. On the other hand, negative spiritual attitudes come from association with the spiritually unhealthy—doubt and deviance are also contagious. Perhaps the worst person to spend too much time with, in depression, is yourself. Don't spend too much time alone. Get out of the house for at least one hour each day.

Research shows that people who attend church or synagogue on a regular basis have a lower risk of mental illness.[3] Rates of depression are lower in people who attend church frequently, and suicide attempts happen less often. A healthy church community can have an antidepressant effect.

Healthy spiritual groups nurture spiritual intimacy and communion. When we share our faith with others, spiritual connections develop through movement of the Holy Spirit. Weblike networks of spiritual intimacy begin to form. Each person's spirit communes individually with God and collectively with each other. The Spirit of God fills one person. The Spirit of God fills another—each one inspired by God's presence in the other as the name of the Lord is lifted up. This is God's family at its best—the movement of the Spirit in His church.

Find a healthy Bible-believing church and get connected. Don't get distracted by the imperfections of people or focus on the hypocrisy we all seem to display at times. Don't assume that because a person goes to church, he or she is moral or even nice. The church is full of people who do wrong things, most of them looking for a better way. And this includes the leaders of each church. While their work usually deserves honor and respect, they also are learning to track with the Spirit. Look past the people in the building and listen for God's message to you.

Spiritual Acceleration

> Why are you downcast, O my soul? Why so disturbed within me? Put your hope in God (Psalm 42:11).

Like a personal diary made public, the Psalms display David's private emotional life. The words above reflect his struggle to hang on to hope in the midst of deep sadness. Little has changed for many people of faith. The following story tells about one woman's private journey from near fatal depression to spiritual exultation.

Staci was a calm and beautiful flight attendant who loved God, cared for her family, did all the right things—but still got depressed. It's hard to say whether chemical imbalances caused conflict with her husband or if her husband's constant criticism triggered chemical imbalance. Either way, Staci became clinically depressed.

She woke each morning in a fog of fear and disgust, and limped her way through the day. Normal ways of thinking ended as depressive ways took over. She felt worthless, helpless, and lost. After one last argument with her husband, she retreated to a bedroom in their basement and took an overdose of sleeping medication.

Early the next morning something prompted her husband to check on her. She would have died if he hadn't put his anger aside and gone down to look. He found her unconscious and called 9-1-1. Hospital doctors admitted her to the ICU, then transferred her to a psychiatric service.

After her release from the hospital, the three of us—Staci, her husband, and I—sat down to sort out what had happened. Over the months preceding her overdose, Staci had slipped away from friends and family, and finally her own good sense. Depression's brain changes caused her to think of herself as an inadequate mother and a bad wife—incapable of a loving relationship.

Feelings of inadequacy gave way to fear. She couldn't stand to be alone, not even for a moment in the bathroom. She was afraid to take a nap because it felt like she was dying. She prayed and read the Bible compulsively, but couldn't control her mounting fear or depression. She was convinced that God had abandoned her and, in her darkest moments, feared she had become possessed by a demon. As she revealed the fright and desperation that had consumed each moment, her reasons for attempting suicide became a bit easier to understand. Desperate ways of thinking had led her to a permanently wrong solution to a temporary illness.

Within two weeks of starting medication, the cloud of depression began to lift from her mind and spirit. As the balance of chemicals in her brain was restored, she discovered how admitting her powerlessness to God provided opportunity for renewal. With enthusiasm and eloquence, she shared her appreciation of His grace and forgiveness. God loved her. He forgave her. Staci wanted me, and anyone else who cared to listen, to know.

She stopped worrying about the future. She trusted God with the best and worst cases she could imagine. Her verbally bitter husband began to mellow. Still, his behavior didn't really matter. Staci was centered on God's love and generosity, assured that regardless of her spouse's behavior, He would keep her in peace. Her husband's threats of divorce lost their sting—God would provide what she needed. His criticism of her care for the children was dismissed. She trusted God and humbly loved her husband—spiritual vitality made it possible.

In time, her family welcomed her back—first the children, then her husband. Staci's compassion paved a way for reconciliation, and her husband sought counseling for his cynical way of thinking.

Between each counseling visit, Staci grew more alive and hungrier to grow closer to the Spirit. Like a rolling snowball, her greater awareness of God's goodness led to more prayer and spiritual searching, then to even greater awareness of His kindness and grace, accelerating her spiritual growth.

Each time we talked, I had the feeling of being pulled along on her adventure, like she was hurrying off to some marvelous place she didn't want me to miss. It was a joy to accompany her along the way. The emotionally exhausted woman who had walked into my office a few weeks earlier now returned each time with delightful vitality. It's funny how counseling, like friendship, can flow both ways—one day you offer hope to your friend, and another day your friend does the same for you.

Staci returned to her friends at church. As she walked into the sanctuary, she heard the congregation reciting Psalm 116:

> The cords of death entangled me;
> the anguish of the grave came upon me;
> I was overcome by trouble and sorrow...
> You have delivered my life from death,
> my eyes from tears.
>
> —Psalm 116:3,8

To Staci, this was a sign of God welcoming her back. She rejoined a church that had grown cold and brought spiritual spontaneity with her. New brothers and sisters asked for her counsel and support in their struggles. She was always quick to remind them and me that her spiritual renewal was not her doing or mine, that grace and acceptance of forgiveness do not come from psychology or medicine.

The Spirit and the Steps

Healing from depression may come through the SMART Steps or some other pathway of God's design. He has His own unique plan for renewing your body, mind, and spirit, starting somewhere along the SMART Steps path. For Staci, renewal blossomed at Step "M." Medication cleared her black moods and enabled her to think through her options with clarity. With clear thinking and mood stability, she was able to work on her relationships with God and her family.

For others, complete spiritual vitality doesn't come until the first four steps are complete. Getting the wrong chemicals out and the right chemicals in restores a person's God-given abilities to find answers to problems. As they work though the steps, they become better able to see their way to God.

Wherever you are in your steps of renewal, pray for guidance and healing, and resolve to love God regardless of outcome. Pray for the strength to take steps that will bring you in line with His will and give you peace in the midst of hardships. May God keep you tracking with His Spirit and give you the power to do the little and great things He has in mind for you.

Action Items

- Ponder Proverbs 3:5-6 and trust God to make your path clear.
- Create a worst-case and best-case scenario list and hand it over to God.
- Take a 30-minute walk out-of-doors. Think over the "Living by Faith" exercise (pages 219–220), applying its power to your worries as you walk.
- Spend time with optimistic believers.
- Think about an interruption to your day. Change your viewpoint. See it as God saying, "Wait. Take some time to pray."
- Purchase a daily devotional or other "bite-sized" collection of Scriptures to ponder.
- For five minutes daily, think deeply upon the name of Yahweh in the manner described in this chapter.
- Put your feet up, relax, and listen to an hour of inspirational music.
- Take all of the necessary steps to become what God has in mind for you to be.

More Helpful
Concepts and Tools

Diagnostic Checklists

Summaries of criteria used in the American Psychiatric Association's diagnostic manual, the DSM-IV

Major depressive disorder:

1. At least five of the following symptoms are present for two weeks or more:

   a. Depressed moods occur most days for most of the day.

   b. Marked decline in pursuit of pleasurable activities nearly every day.

   c. Greater than 5 percent change in body weight in one month.

   d. Excessive sleep or lack of sleep every night.

   e. Appears agitated or lethargic every day.

   f. Reports low energy most days.

   g. Feels worthless or inappropriate guilt most days.

   h. Concentration problems nearly every day.

   i. Recurrent wish to be dead.

2. Symptoms listed above cause significant decline in functioning at home or work.

3. Symptoms are not due to substance abuse or direct effect of general medical illness.

Bipolar disorder, depressed:

1. Presently experiencing a Major Depressive Episode (as defined above).

2. There has been at least one *manic episode* as defined below:

   a. Period of at least one week in which mood is persistently and abnormally elevated, expansive, or irritable. May be less than one week if hospitalization is required.

   b. During this one-week period, three or more of the following symptoms have been persistently noticeable:

      i. Grandiosity or inflated self-esteem

      ii. Decreased desire to sleep (for example, person feels rested with three hours of sleep)

      iii. Increased rate and amount of speech

      iv. Feels like thoughts are racing or jumps between topics

      v. Highly distractible

      vi. Increased activity (for example work, sex, social)

      vii. Impulsive pleasure activities or foolish business risks

   c. Mood changes cause impairments with work or relationships.

Premenstrual dysphoric disorder *(while not an established DSM-IV diagnosis, this disorder is being considered for inclusion in a later edition):*

1. In most of the menstrual cycles of the past year, five or more of the following were present in the week before menstruation

but absent after completion of menses. Symptoms must include at least one of items a, b, c, or d.

   a. Marked depressed mood

   b. Significant increase in tension or feeling "keyed up"

   c. Sudden periods of sadness or sensitivity to rejection

   d. Marked anger or interpersonal conflicts

   e. Decreased interest in usual activities

   f. Difficulty concentrating

   g. Low energy

   h. Marked change in appetite

   i. Marked increase or decrease in sleep

   j. Feeling overwhelmed

   k. Physical symptoms such as bloating or breast tenderness

2. Mood changes interfere with work or social relationships

3. Symptoms are not simply the worsening of another depressive disorder

Items 1-3 must be confirmed by daily ratings for at least two consecutive cycles.

Adjustment disorder depression:

1. Onset of emotional or behavioral symptoms within three months of a clearly identifiable stressor (for example, job loss or end of romantic relationship).

2. Symptoms are greater than normally expected from the stressor, or function in workplace or family is significantly impaired.

3. Symptoms do not persist more than six months following end of stressful event.

Signs of Alcohol Dependence

In the past 12 months, have you...

Yes ❑   No ❑   developed tolerance (needed more alcohol to get same effect)?

Yes ❑   No ❑   shown signs of withdrawal (insomnia or agitation)?

Yes ❑   No ❑   drunk more than you intended?

Yes ❑   No ❑   failed at attempts to cut down?

Yes ❑   No ❑   spent less time on nondrinking activities?

Yes ❑   No ❑   continued to drink despite medical or mental-health problems?

Three or more "yes" answers suggests alcohol dependence.

These questions may be used to assess other destructive habits.

The checklists in this appendix are based on *American Psychiatric Association: Diagnostic and Statistical Manual of Mental Disorders,* 4th ed. (Washington, DC: American Psychiatric Association Press Text Revision, 2000).

"The Glove"

*A model for understanding the mind,
body, and spirit relationship*

- The *body* is natural. It follows the natural laws of chemistry and physics. But a human being is more than chemicals reacting in a sea of protoplasm. The body is a beautifully designed resting place for the soul, a passive dwelling space for a creative spirit.

- The *spirit* is supernatural. It isn't part of the body. It eludes description by human language, defies the laws of nature, and can be known only through its reflection in our minds. It is the spirit that communes with God and permits supernatural experience.

- The *mind* is the interface of body and spirit—the place where supernatural spirit influences the natural body and where physical illness can produce spiritual suffering. In depressive illness, the mind can be influenced by changes in the body, and it can alter our spiritual perception.

"The glove." I believe the complex interaction of body, mind, and spirit can be best described by using a simple picture. Conceptually, the mind can be viewed as a glove, the spirit as a hand within the glove, and the brain as the stuff manipulated by the gloved hand. A hand working within a glove is like the spirit working within the mind.

Consider the hand of a neurosurgeon operating on someone's brain. As the hand moves within the glove, we see the glove move. The glove makes changes in the brain. Although we cannot see the hand, we know it is there.

In a similar way, the spirit moves the mind, and the mind produces changes in the brain. We can watch brain chemistry changes with specialized instruments, but we cannot see the spirit that causes the chemical reaction.

The glove of depression. Some gloves are thick and bulky. Others are made from a thin and flexible film. Thick cotton gloves, for instance, are nearly useless to a neurosurgeon. Aside from concerns about sterility, a thick cotton glove prevents the surgeon from feeling what is going on at his fingertips. He can't appreciate the finer structures in the tissue.

Depression is like a thick cotton glove. This "mind glove" makes it hard to work or feel the pleasure of living. The spirit, operating within a mind and body altered by depression, can't feel happy over good news. Depression causes a person to feel insulated from God and separated from intimate relationship.

In recovery, the thick cotton glove needs to be replaced with a thin latex one. With the removal of the bulky and cumbersome "mind glove" of depression, the spirit is free to move things around...and appreciate the touch of a friend.

Tools

Stress-management activities
Relaxation techniques
Eight tips for sleeping better
FDA-approved antidepressant medications
Scripture verses to give you hope
Internet resources

Stress-Management Activities

Body:

- *Sleep.* Give your brain time to rebalance. Several weeks of poor sleep can lead to depression. Several days of good sleep can help start your recovery.

- *Rest.* Take one full day of rest every week—avoid as many responsibilities as you can on that day. It's your day to regain spiritual perspective and indulge your need for recreation.

- *Exercise* releases physical stress and helps blow off steam. Talk to your doctor before beginning more aggressive routines.

- *Eat well.* Your brain needs nutrients to repair broken brain cells. Eat more fruits and vegetables and protein products. Drink at least two quarts of water each day.

- *Replace a habit* of substance abuse with a healthy new behavior. Alcohol and illicit drugs increase depressive symptoms and interfere with treatment.

Mind:

- *Get out of the house* for at least one hour per day. It will change your perspective and distract your mind from negative ways of thinking.
- *Have fun.* Start a hobby. A few moments painting, drawing, or making music allow expression of deeper emotion and stir creative thinking.
- *Talk to a friend.* Ask her to go shopping. Ask him to meet you for coffee.
- *Call a family member.* She may be a source of encouragement and hands-on help.
- *Go to your bookshelf* and find a book that once gave you joy.
- *Practice relaxation techniques.*

Spirit:

- *Pray.* Praise God. Confess and ask for forgiveness. Then pray for someone else.
- *Make a worry list* and give it to God.
- *Find a church.* Show up.
- *Listen* to inspirational music for one hour.
- *Visit a bookstore.* Find and read an inspirational book— perhaps a new Bible or daily devotional.
- *Join a group* of supportive people who can help you stay focused on spiritual ways to healing.
- *Give to others.* Find a worthy cause and volunteer some time.

Relaxation Techniques

As you move through the day your body collects tension. If this tension isn't released, your body may protest through *psychosomatic* symptoms—your *psyche* (mind) and your *soma* (body) get sick together. Stomachaches may say it's time to take some time off. Headaches may tell you to find some quiet time for yourself. A pain in the neck may be telling you to avoid that difficult relationship for a while. Learning to live in peace requires developing the ability to relax in the midst of challenging circumstances. Use one of these relaxation techniques at least once each day.

Slow deep breathing (short technique #1):

1. Find a quiet time and place to relax for a few moments.
2. Close your eyes and begin a series of slow deep breaths. Fill your lungs with as much air as you can hold, then slowly exhale through your nose. Resist the temptation to speed up the process with rapid shallow breaths.
3. Concentrate on each breath. Let stressful thoughts go away with each exhaled breath.
4. Continue the process for a while.

Meditation (short technique #2):

1. Begin with the slow-deep-breathing technique above.
2. With each slowly inhaled breath, say to yourself a short phrase (see suggestions in chart).
3. With each slowly exhaled breath, say to yourself a short phrase (see chart). Pick one pair of inhale-exhale phrases and repeat it several times.

Inhale ⟶	Exhale
Thank you,	Jesus
The Lord is	my shepherd
Yah -	weh
Holy Spirit,	come

Visualization (short technique #3):

1. Begin with the slow-deep-breathing technique above.

2. Picture yourself in a relaxing place—maybe a childhood vacation spot or another place you'd like to be, such as a cool mountain meadow or a warm, sunny beach.

3. Spend some time feeling the breeze, smelling the fresh air, and appreciating the beauty around you. As best as you're able, stay there for a few moments as you continue to breath slowly and deeply, allowing each cleansing breath to carry you deeper into that relaxing place.

Progressive muscle relaxation (long technique). Begin your progressive muscle relaxation (PMR) experience by finding a quiet place to relax for 5 to 10 minutes—maybe your easy chair or bed. Make yourself comfortable. Close your eyes and take several slow deep breaths. It may be helpful to imagine yourself lying on a thick feather mattress, with the mattress caressing your body.

Now begin thinking about the way you're breathing. Slow it down now. Make your breathing slower and deeper. Every time you inhale, make your breath slow and deep. Every time you exhale, let the air move out very slowly. Do this for a while. Being patient is helpful. Focus on the air passing in and out of your nostrils and filling your lungs. Repeat this procedure for about one minute.

Next, begin a process of stress–rest cycling—progressively relaxing your body's muscles. PMR is a step-by-step process of contracting and relaxing large groups of muscles as you keep focused on the process of slow and deep breathing. You will begin to focus on the upper body, then move to your lower body, and then to your whole body.

1. *Facial muscles.* While resting in your comfortable place, take a deep breath and contract the muscles of your face. Hold your breath for five seconds as you tightly close your eyes, clench your jaws, and scrunch up your facial muscles. Then slowly

exhale as you relax all of your muscles. Continue a process of slow, deep cleansing breaths for a moment.

2. *Upper body.* Next, repeat the cycle of stress and relaxation with the upper half of your body. Take a deep breath and hold it for five seconds as you contract muscles of your face, neck and shoulders, arms and hands. Keep your upper body tense for five seconds. Then slowly exhale as you let your body rest. Continue to breathe slowly and deeply.

3. *Full body.* Finally, put your whole body through a cycle of stress and rest. Take a deep breath and contract every muscle you can. Grit your teeth. Make two fists and curl up the toes of your feet. Let your body be as stressed as it can be—uptight, rigid, and full of tension. Then slowly let the air pass out of your nostrils as you allow each tiny muscle of your body to relax.

Remain in this place of rest for a while. This state of relaxation may be a good time for spiritual thinking—for prayer or meditation on inspirational ideas. Continue the pattern of slow cleansing breaths until it is time to get up.

You can use PMR to get to sleep after a stressful day. You can take a few moments of deliberate slow deep breathing in the car before a job interview or blind date. Relaxing your body will empower your mind to operate at its highest potential.

Eight Tips for Sleeping Better

Sleep is barometer of mental health. People who are sleeping well are usually feeling and thinking quite well. Those who are struggling with mental health are almost always having difficulty getting good sleep.

Lack of sleep is a major risk factor for depression and a classic symptom of depression. Guidelines for sleep generally recommend 6 to 10 hours of sleep each night. In times of recovery from depression 8 to 10 hours may be better, allowing more time for the brain to heal and the mind to release worries.

Find some healthy ways to sleep while it's dark and be awake while it's light. This is how your body was created to operate. Here are a few tips for better sleep:

1. *Exercise most days of the week.* Many people find that regular exercise is a requirement for good sleep. Try to exercise at least three hours before bedtime. Working out too close to bedtime may make it hard to settle down.

2. *Try a little prayer and meditation or a relaxation technique* before bedtime.

3. *Avoid foods high in sugar.* These can make it hard to wind down. Reduce or eliminate drinks with caffeine. Even one cup of coffee in the morning can impair the ability to sleep in some people.

4. *Abstain from alcohol.* Alcohol may have initial sedative effects but can cause rebound insomnia several hours later. It also interferes with medical and counseling treatments of depression.

5. *Avoid nicotine.* Nicotine use around bedtime can interfere with sleep.

6. *Establish a regular bedtime.* Limit daytime sleep if it causes a disruption to nighttime rest. A full night of sleep tonight will make it much easier to deal with the challenges of tomorrow.

7. *Make your bedroom conducive to sleep.* It should be dark, cool, and quiet. Find pillows and bed coverings that are comfortable

for you. If your spouse snores, you may need to sleep in another room until you establish a sleep schedule for your body.

8. *Consider medical evaluation if sleep problems persist.* Serious insomnia may warrant medical treatment. Conditions such as restless leg syndrome and sleep apnea may rob you of necessary rest.

FDA-Approved Antidepressant Medications
Including generic names and brand names

Selective serotonin reuptake inhibitors (SSRIs):
Citalopram	*Celexa**
Escitalopram	*Lexapro*
Fluoxetine	*Prozac, Sarafem*
Fluvoxamine	*Luvox*
Paroxetine	*Paxil, Paxil CR, Pexeva*
Sertraline	*Zoloft*

Serotonin norepinephrine reuptake inhibitors:
Duloxetine	*Cymbalta*
Venlafaxine	*Effexor, Effexor XR*
Desvenlafaxine	*Pristiq*

Heterocyclic compounds:
Amitriptyline	*Elavil*
Clomipramine	*Anafranil*
Desipramine	*Norpramin*
Doxepin	*Sinequan*
Imipramine	*Tofranil*
Nortriptyline	*Aventyl, Pamelor*
Protriptyline	*Vivactil*

Monoamine oxidase inhibitors:
Isocarboxazid	*Marplan*
Phenelzine	*Nardil*
Selegiline	*Emsam*
Tranylcypromine	*Parnate*

Other antidepressants:
Bupropion	*Aplenzia, Wellbutrin, Wellbutrin SR, Wellbutrin XL*
Mirtazapine	*Remeron, Remeron SolTab*
Trazodone	*Desyrel*

---

* Italics indicate brand names.

Scripture Verses to Give You Hope

Be strong and take heart, all you who hope in the LORD.

—Psalm 31:24

Why are you downcast, O my soul? Why so disturbed within me? Put your hope in God, for I will yet praise him, my Savior and my God.

—Psalm 42:11

Come to me, all you who are weary and burdened, and I will give you rest.

—Jesus, in Matthew 11:28

I have told you these things, so that in me you may have peace. In this world you will have trouble. But take heart! I have overcome the world.

—Jesus, in John 16:33

Cast your cares upon the LORD and he will sustain you; he will never let the righteous fall.

—Psalm 55:22

Do not be anxious about anything, but in everything, by prayer and petition, with thanksgiving, present your requests to God. And the peace of God, which transcends all understanding, will guard your hearts and minds in Christ Jesus.

—Philippians 4:6-7

God is our refuge and strength, an ever-present help in time of trouble.

—Psalm 46:1

We know that in all things God works for the good of those who love him, who have been called according to his purpose.

—Romans 8:28

The LORD himself goes before you and will be with you; he will never leave you nor forsake you. Do not be afraid; do not be discouraged.

—DEUTERONOMY 31:8

Those who hope in the LORD will renew their strength. They will soar on wings like eagles; they will run and not grow weary, they will walk and not be faint.

—ISAIAH 40:31

Internet Resources

Medical and psychological organizations:
    American Psychiatric Association: www.psych.org
    American Psychological Association: www.apa.org
    American Association for Marriage and Family Therapy:
        www.aamft.org

Christian mental-health services:
    Focus on the Family: www.focusonthefamily.org
    Meier Clinics: www.MeierClinics.org
    New Life Ministries: www.newlife.com
    American Association of Christian Counselors: www.AACC.net
    Christian Medical and Dental Associations: www.cmdahome.org
    American Association of Pastoral Counselors: www.aapc.org

Depression information:
    National Mental Health Association: www.depression-screening.org
    All About Depression: http://allaboutdepression.com
    Mental Health Channel: www.mentalhealthchannel.net/depression
        /index.shtml
    National Institute of Health: www.nimh.nih.gov/publicat
        /depressionmenu.cfm
    National Library of Medicine: www.nlm.nih.gov
    National Foundation for Depressive Illness: www.depression.org

Patient support and advocacy groups:
    National Depressive and Manic Depressive Association:
        www.ndmda.org
    National Alliance for the Mentally Ill: www.nami.org

Notes

....

Index

Notes

Chapter 1—The Big Picture

1. R.H. Belmaker and G. Agam, "Major Depressive Disorders," *New England Journal of Medicine,* 358:55, 2008.

2. James Dobson, *When God Doesn't Make Sense* (Wheaton, IL: Tyndale House, 1993).

3. American Psychiatric Association, *Diagnostic and Statistical Manual of Mental Disorders,* 4th ed. text rev. (Washington, DC: American Psychiatric Association, 2000).

4. Elizabeth Skoglund, *Bright Days Dark Nights: With Charles Spurgeon in Triumph over Emotional Pain* (Grand Rapids, MI: Baker Books, 2000).

5. Justin Ewers, "The Real Abraham Lincoln," *US News and World Report,* February 21, 2005; R.W. Hudgens, "Mental Health of Political Candidates: Notes on Abraham Lincoln," *American Journal of Psychiatry* (1973) 130:110.

6. William Styron, *Darkness Visible: A Memoir of Madness* (Toronto: Random House of Canada Limited, 1990).

Chapter 2—The Black-Mood Brain

1. Benjamin Sadock and Virginia Sadock, eds., *Kaplan and Sadock's Comprehensive Textbook of Psychiatry VII* (Philadelphia: Lippincott, Williams and Wilkins, 2000).

2. J.D. Bremner, M. Vythilingam, et al., "MRI and PET Study of Deficits in Hippocampal Structure and Function in Women with Childhood Sexual Abuse and Post-traumatic Stress Disorder," *American Journal of Psychiatry,* (2003) 160:924-932.

3. D.J. Kupfer, "Long-term Treatment of Depression," *Journal of Clinical Psychiatry,* 52, suppl. 28-34, 1991.

4. Sadock and Sadock, eds.

5. H.L. Urry, C.M. van Reekum, et al., "Amygdala and Ventromedial Prefrontal Cortex are Inversely Coupled," *Neuroscience,* (2006) 26:4415-4425.

6. J. Keller, L. Shen, et al., "Hippocampal and Amygdalar Volume in Psychotic and Nonpsychotic Unipolar Depression," *American Journal of Psychiatry,* (2008) 165:7.

7. P. Gold and D. Charney, "Diseases of the Mind, Brain, and Body," *American Journal of Psychiatry* (2002) 159:1826.

8. T.S. Frodl, N. Koutsouleris, et al., "Depression-Related Variation in Brain Morphology over 3 Years," *Archives of General Psychiatry* (2008) 65:1156-1165.

9. Sadock and Sadock, eds.

10. M. Wylie, "Visionary or Voodoo," *Psychotherapy Networker,* September/October (2005): 36-68.

Chapter 3—Hormone Havoc

1. K. Fackelmann, "Stress can ravage the body, unless the mind says no," USAToday.com. March 21, 2005.

2. Paul Meier, Todd Clements, et al., *Blue Genes: Breaking Free from the Chemical Imbalances that Affect Your Moods, Your Mind, Your Life, and Your Loved Ones* (Wheaton, IL: Tyndale House Publishers, 2005).

3. American Psychiatric Association, *Diagnostic and Statistical Manual of Mental Disorders,* 4th ed. (Washington, DC: American Psychiatric Association, 2000).

4. Archibald Hart and Catherine Hart Weber, *Stressed or Depressed: A Practical and Inspirational Guide for Parents of Hurting Teens* (Nashville: Integrity Publishers, 2005).

5. K.M. Husseini, J.A. Quiroz, D. Charney, et al., "Enhancing Neuronal Plasticity and Cellular Resilience to Develop Novel, Improved Therapeutics for Difficult-to-Treat Depression," *Biological Psychiatry* (2003) 53:707-742.

6. D.P. Hall, "Stress, Suicide, and Military Service During Operation Uphold Democracy," *Military Medicine* (1996) 161:159-163.

7. D.P. Hall, "A Widow's Grief: Language of the Heart," *Journal of the American Medical Association* (1992) 268:871-872.

8. Benjamin Sadock and Virginia Sadock, eds., *Kaplan and Sadock's Comprehensive Textbook of Psychiatry VII* (Philadelphia: Lippincott, Williams & Wilkins, 2000).

9. G.E. Tafet, V.P. Idoyaga-Vargas, et al., "Correlation Between Cortisol Level and Serotonin Uptake in Patients with Chronic Stress and Depression," *Cognitive and Affective Behavioral Neuroscience,* (2001) 1:388-93; B.S. McEwen and A.M. Magarinos, "Stress and Hippocampal Plasticity: Implications for Pathophysiology of Affective Disorders," *HumanPsychopharmacology,* (2001) 16(S1):S7-S19; R.M. Sapolsky, "Glucocorticoids and Hippocampal Atrophy in Neuropsychiatric Disorders," *Archives of General Psychiatry* (2000) 57:925-935.

10. R.S. Duman, "Depression: A Case of Neuronal Life or Death?" *Biological Psychiatry* (2004) 56:140-145; E. Shimizu, K. Hashimoto, and M. Iyo, "Major Depressive Disorders and BDNF (Brain Derived Neurotrophic Factor)," *Nihon Shinkei Seishin Yakurigaku Zasshi* (2004) 24:147-150.

11. F. Karege, G. Perret, et al., "Decreased Serum Brain-Derived Neurotrophic Factor Levels in Major Depression Patients," *Psychiatric Research* (2002) 109:143-148.

12. Duman; E. Shimizu, K. Hashimoto, et al., "Alterations of Serum Levels of Brain-Derived

Neurotrophic Factor (BDNF) in Depressed Patients With or Without Antidepressants," *Biological Psychiatry,* (2003) 54:70-75; H. Manev, T. Uz, et al., "Antidepressants Alter Cell Proliferation in the Adult Brain In-vivo and in Neural Cultures In-vitro," *European Journal of Psychopharmacology,* (2001) 411:67-70.

13. Sadock and Sadock, eds.

Chapter 4—Mood-Messenger Misfire

1. Alfred Gillman, Louis Goodman, et al., *Goodman and Gillman's The Pharmacological Basis of Therapeutics* (New York: MacMillan, 1985).

2. J. Borg, B. Andree, et al., "The Serotonin System and Spiritual Experience," *American Journal of Psychiatry,* (2003) 160:1955-1969.

3. C.A. Stockmeier et al., "Increase in Serotonin 1A Auto Receptors in the Midbrain of Suicide Victims with Major Depression—Post Mortem Evidence for Decreased Serotonin Activity," *Journal of Neuroscience,* September 15; 18(18): 7394-401.

4. Borg, Andree, et al.

Chapter 5—The Inheritance of Dark Moods

1. A. Caspi, K. Sugden, T.E. Moffitt, et al., "Influence of Life Stress on Depression: Moderation by a Polymorphism in the 5-HTT Gene," *Science* (2003), 301:386-389.

2. American Psychiatric Association, *Diagnostic and Statistical Manual of Mental Disorders,* 4th ed. (Washington, DC: American Psychiatric Association, 2000).

3. Benjamin Sadock and Virginia Sadock, eds., *Kaplan and Sadock's Comprehensive Textbook of Psychiatry VII* (Philadelphia: Lippincott, Williams and Wilkins, 2000).

Chapter 7—Repression and the Unconscious

1. Sigmund Freud, *The Standard Edition of the Complete Psychological Works of Sigmund Freud,* tr. James Strachey (London: Hogarth Press Ltd., 1959).

2. C.S. Lewis, *Mere Christianity* (New York: MacMillan Publishing Co, 1952).

3. M.C. Anderson and C. Green, "Suppressing Unwanted Memories by Executive Control," *Nature* (2001), 410:366-369.

Chapter 8—Problems of Spiritual Personality

1. H.G. Koenig, D.G. Cohen, et al., "Religious Coping and Depression Among Elderly Hospitalized Medically Ill Men," *American Journal of Psychiatry,* (1992) 149, 1693-1700.

2. E. Paykel, J. Myers, et al., "Suicidal Feelings in the General Population: A Prevalence Study," *British Journal of Psychiatry,* 124 (1974): 460-69; G.M. Comstock, K.B. Partridge, "Church Attendance and Health," *Journal of Chronic Diseases,* 25 (1972): 665-72.

3. C.S. Lewis, *The Screwtape Letters* (New York: Bantam Books, 1982).

4. Chuck Smith, *Why Grace Changes Everything* (Costa Mesa CA: The Word for Today, 2007).

Chapter 9—Recognizing Depression as an Illness

1. Frank Minirth and Paul Meier, *Happiness Is a Choice* (Grand Rapids, MI: Baker Books, 1994).

2. Peter Kramer, *Against Depression* (New York: Viking Penguin, 2005).

Chapter 10—Finding Someone to Help

1. Gordon Allport, *The Individual and His Religion* (New York: Macmillan, 1953).

2. A. Ellis, "Psychotherapy and Atheistic Values: A Response to A. Bergin's 'Psychotherapy and Religious Values,'" *Journal of Consulting and Clinical Psychology,* (1980) 48:635-39.

3. Sigmund Freud, *The Standard Edition of Complete Psychological Works of Sigmund Freud* (London: Hogarth Press, 1953-1974).

4. American Psychiatric Association, "The Public's View," *Psychiatric News,* May 6, 2005: 1, 15.

5. A.E. Bergin and J.P. Jensen, "Religiosity of Psychotherapists National Survey," *Psychotherapy,* 27: 3-7.

6. "Guidelines Regarding Possible Conflict Between Psychiatrists' Religious Commitments and Psychiatric Practice," *American Psychiatric Association Document Reference 890011,* December 1989.

7. American Association of Christian Counselors, *Christian Counseling Connection,* page 20, Issue 2, 2004.

8. For examples of such approaches, see Terry Wardle, *Wounded: How You Can Find Inner Wholeness and Healing in Him* (Camp Hill, PA: Christian Publications, 1994); John Sanford and Paula Sanford, *Healing the Wounded Spirit* (Tulsa, OK: Victory House, 1985); Edward Smith, *Healing Life's Deepest Hurts* (Ventura, CA: Regal Books, 2002).

9. Elvin Stanton, *Cancer: Faith over Fear* (Montgomery, AL: New Voice Publishing, 2007).

Chapter 11—Symptoms and Diagnosis

1. American Psychiatric Association, *Diagnostic and Statistical Manual of Mental Disorders,* 4th ed. (Washington, DC: American Psychiatric Association, 2000).

Chapter 13—Stop Substance Abuse

1. American Psychiatric Association *Diagnostic and Statistical Manual of Mental Disorders,* 4th ed. (Washington, DC: American Psychiatric Association, 2000).

2. R.M. Swift, "Drug Therapy for Alcohol Dependence," *New England Journal of Medicine,* (1999); 340: 1482-1490.

3. F. Tims, C. Leukefeld, and J. Platt, eds., *Relapse and Recovery in Addictions* (New Haven: Yale University Press, 2001).

4. *Twelve Steps and Twelve Traditions* (New York: Alcoholics Anonymous World Services, Inc., 1981).

5. *Living Sober* (New York: Alcoholics Anonymous World Services, Inc., 1998).

6. National Institute on Alcohol Abuse and Alcoholism (NIAAA), *Helping Patients Who Drink Too Much: A Clinician's Guide* (Bethesda, MD: National Institutes of Health, 2005).

Chapter 14—Medicate Chemical Imbalances

1. L. Lamberg, "Athletes Not Invincible When It Comes to Mental Illness," *Psychiatric News,* July 20, 2001.

2. *Physicians Desk Reference* (Montvale, NJ: Thompson PDR, 2006).

3. A.J. Rush, J. Kilner, et al., "Clinically Relevant Findings from STAR*D," *Psychiatric Annals,* March 2008, 38:3; M. Fava and S. Targum, "Augmentation and Combination Strategies to Treat the Residual Symptoms of Major Depressive Disorder," *Psychiatry,* February 2007.

Chapter 15—Adjust Expectations of Yourself

1. Robert McGee, *The Search for Significance* (Houston: Rapha Publishing, 1990).

2. Frank Minirth and Paul Meier, *Happiness Is a Choice* (Grand Rapids, MI: Baker Books, 1994).

Chapter 16—Revise Relationships with Others

1. Ray Linder, *What Will I Do with My Money?: How Personality Affects Your Financial Behavior* (Chicago: Northfield Publishing, 2000).

2. Henry Cloud and John Townsend, *Boundaries* (Grand Rapids: Zondervan, 1992).

3. Gary Chapman, *The Five Love Languages* (Chicago: Northfield Publishing, 1992).

4. M. Iacoboni, "Face-to-face: The neural basis of social mirroring and empathy," *Psychiatric Annals.* (2007) 37:4.

5. Larry Crabb, *Soul Talk* (Nashville: Integrity Publishers, 2003).

Chapter 17—Track with the Holy Spirit

1. "Living by Faith," words by James Wells, 1918.

2. Jeffery Sheler, "The Power of Prayer," *US News and World Report,* December 20, 2004.

3. Dale Matthews and Connie Clark, *The Faith Factor* (New York: Viking, 1998).

Index

About the Author

Don Hall is a counseling psychiatrist and the practice manager of Riverside Counseling Center in Leesburg, Virginia. He enjoys exploring connections between psychiatry and spirituality and integrating these insights into care for his patients.

A graduate of Georgetown University School of Medicine and a diplomate of the American Board of Psychiatry and Neurology, Dr. Hall has worked with medication-development researchers at Georgetown and the National Institutes of Health. He was awarded the American Psychiatric Association's Resident Research Award for work on depression conducted at Johns Hopkins Hospital.

After medical school, Dr. Hall entered the army, attaining the rank of major. He served as psychiatrist for the 82nd Airborne Division and was later was appointed Chief of Outpatient Psychiatry at Walter Reed Army Medical Center. As a clinical assistant professor of psychiatry at the Uniformed Services University of Health Sciences, he published two psychiatric handbooks and authored over 20 medical-journal articles, including reports in the *American Journal of Psychiatry* and *Journal of the American Medical Association*.

Now in private practice, Dr. Hall continues to explore connections between faith and medicine through stimulating conversations with patients and review of brain science research reports. *Breaking Through Depression* is his first book for Harvest House Publishers.

www.donhallmd.com

Harvest House Resources for
Physical, Emotional, and Spiritual Health

Overcoming Runaway Blood Sugar

Practical Help for • People Fighting Fatigue and Mood Swings • Hypoglycemics and Diabetics • Those Trying to Control Their Weight

Dennis Pollock

With this positive, can-do approach, you can gain maximum health while losing excess pounds. You'll discover...

- why runaway blood sugar is a key factor in food cravings and weight issues
- how blood-sugar problems lead to damage to your body
- ways to evaluate pre-diabetes health risks, such as hypoglycemia
- diet and exercise that really work

Whether you are diabetic, have a family history of diabetes, or are simply tired of being sick and tired, *Overcoming Runaway Blood Sugar* may very well change the way you view eating and exercise forever.

......

Overcoming Back and Neck Pain

A Proven Program for Recovery and Prevention

Lisa Morrone, PT

From 20 years of teaching and practicing physical therapy, Lisa Morrone gives you a way to say *no* to the treadmill of prescriptions, endless treatments, and a limited lifestyle. This straightforward, clinically proven approach shows you how to...

- benefit from good posture and "core stability"
- strengthen and stretch key muscles
- shift to healthy movement patterns
- recover from pain caused by compressed or degenerated discs
- address "inside issues" that affect healing—nutrition, rest, and emotional/spiritual struggles

The Emotionally Destructive Relationship

Seeing It, Stopping It, Surviving It

Leslie Vernick

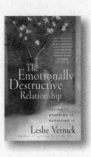

Stop. Dare to ask the question:
What's going wrong in this relationship?

Maybe it doesn't seem to be "abuse." No bruises, no sexual viola-tion. Even smiles on the surface. Nonetheless, before your eyes, a person is being destroyed emotionally. Perhaps that person is someone you want to help. Perhaps it's you.

Step by step, author and counselor Leslie Vernick guides you on how to...

- recognize behaviors that are meant to control, punish, and hurt
- confront and speak truth when the timing is right
- determine when to keep trying and when to shift your approach
- get safe and stay safe
- continue to be transformed by God

Do you want to change? Within the pages of this book, you will find biblically sound, straightforward help to take the first step today.

······

Becoming Who God Intended

A New Picture for Your Past • A Healthy Way of Managing Your Emotions
A Fresh Perspective on Relationships

David Eckman

Whether you realize it or not, your imagination is filled with *pictures* of reality. The Bible indicates these pictures reveal your true "heart beliefs"—the beliefs that actually shape your every-day feelings and reactions.

David Eckman compassionately shows you how to allow God's Spirit to build new, *biblical* pictures in your heart and imagina-tion. As you do this, you will be able to experience the life God the Father has always intended for you.

> "David Eckman is a man you can trust...His teaching resonates
> with God's wisdom and compassion."
>
> —STU WEBER, author of *Tender Warrior* and *Four Pillars of a Man's Heart*